Date Due

APR 2 5			
	PRINTED	IN U. S. A.	

STUDIES IN MODERN EUROPEAN LITERATURE
AND THOUGHT

General Editor:
E R I C H H E L L E R
Professor of German
in the University College of Swansea

H Ö L D E R L I N

HÖLDERLIN

BY

L. S. SALZBERGER

NEW HAVEN

YALE UNIVERSITY PRESS

1952

831.6
H71 Ys1
Ys1

CONTENTS

49612

I

Introduction

The early part of the nineteenth century was an age of re-orient-
ation. In the writers of that time there began to appear a deepening sense of responsibility, an impulse towards 'the investig-
ation of the indwelling and living ground of all things'(Coleridge,
Biographia Literaria). Hölderlin, who began writing towards
the end of the eighteenth century, had his part to play in this
movement. His first concern was with the nature and function
of the poet, and in his work the poet becomes the crucial subject
of poetry. His ideal poet is no Pygmalion in love with his own
creation; Hölderlin was not a believer in art for art's sake, but in
art for the sake of civilisation and the human soul.

Wordsworth, who was unknown to Hölderlin, though they
were born in the same year, described the poet as 'the rock of
defence of human nature, an upholder and preserver . . . binding
together the vast empire of human society'. Hölderlin would
have accepted this view whole-heartedly, though he would have
felt that it did not go far enough. With his belief in the prophetic mission of poetry, and in the poet as the High Priest of his
people, he was more akin to Blake than to Wordsworth. Like
Blake, he saw the poet as custodian of the past and architect of
the future. But the parallel between the English and the German
visionaries ends here. Temperamentally they were dissimilar.
Hölderlin lacked Blake's luminous serenity and his complete
faith in the Christian tradition. He felt himself to be living in an
age in which there were no longer any universally accepted values, an age crippling to the spirit of the poet.

Hölderlin's dilemma was that of the poet of our own day. Like
Mr T. S. Eliot, he saw

> The broken standards, the broken lives
> The broken faith in one place or another (*The Rock*)

On the one hand it seemed to him that the very ground was
taken from under the poet's feet and that he could not, in such
conditions, fulfil his true mission. On the other hand he believed
that the whole burden of re-vitalising faith fell upon the shoul-
ders of the poet, who, at all times, was the devinely appointed
prophet of mankind. His overvaluation of the poet's mission
was the outcome of that very spiritual disintegration which his
song laments.

7

Hölderlin's poetry is the battlefield on which this conflict is fought out. All his life he wrestled with gods and men to pluck inspiration out of their hearts. He was like Jacob, wrestling with the angel and crying out: 'I will not let thee go except thou bless me'. Hölderlin, however, never received the blessing he sought; he did not have the gift of prophecy; but he was granted vision, true holiness and the power of words. The elemental innocence of his language and the concrete yet ethereal quality of his mature work are unique in the history of German literature, and rare in the poetry of any time and any nation.

II

The Background

Ist also dies die heilige Bahn?
Herrlicher Blick - O trüge mich nicht!
Diese geh' ich? schwebend auf des Liedes
Hoher fliegender Morgenwolke? [1]

These lines, written by Johann Christian Friedrich Hölderlin when he was seventeen, express the awe and rapture of a young man in love with the poetic ideal. At this time he was still a pupil at the Monastery School of Maulbronn, in the German Duchy of Württemberg.

Hölderlin was born on March 20th, 1770, in Lauffen, a small town in Württemberg, but spent most of his childhood in the neighbouring town of Nürtingen. His father died when he was two years old. His mother married again, but lost her second husband when Hölderlin was nine. She had, in all, three children; Friedrich and a younger daughter by her first husband, and one son by her second. Hölderlin was an affectionate boy, deeply attached to his mother, younger sister and half-brother. The mother, a kind, simple and very pious woman, brought up her children in the orthodox Lutheran faith. It was her intention that her eldest son should follow in the footsteps of his father by entering the service of the Church. It was very natural that she should favour this course, for not only would Hölderlin thus be carrying on the family tradition but, since all theological training was paid for by the State, his education would no longer be a charge upon her

[1] English translations of passages quoted in the text will be found on pages 61-64.

slender resources. Accordingly at the age of fourteen Hölderlin was sent to the Monastery School of Denkendorf. After two years he went on to the more advanced and better known School of Maulbronn. From 1788 to 1793 he studied at the celebrated Theological Seminary of Tübingen.

But much to his mother's sorrow, Hölderlin was not to enter the Church. Even as a schoolboy he hated the prospect. He was sensitive, and suffered acutely under the strict discipline to which he was subjected. Above all, he simply could not see himself as a parson. He had one great ambition–to become a poet. It is important to note, however, that while he was resolved to abandon the Church, he was yet convinced of his religious vocation. His *holy way*–an expression borrowed from Isaiah–was not the way of the theologian but of the poet. For him, the poet was the true priest, the prophet, the intermediary between God and man.

This conception of the poet as priest has a venerable history, going back to primitive times when the diverse functions of physician, lawgiver, priest and poet were all vested in a single individual. This multiplicity of function seems to have survived to some extent in the highly developed ancient civilisations of Judea and Greece. The Hebrew prophet was religious leader, politician, legislator and sometimes physician to his people. Having regard to his unsurpassed power of expression, he might also be looked upon as their poet. The Greek poet, certainly, was revered as a moral teacher. Hesiod, Pindar and the Greek tragedians were held to be messengers of divine wisdom.

Hölderlin's imagination was fired by the ideal of the poet fashioned in the image of these divinely inspired teachers of the past. He was steeped in biblical and classical literature. Indeed, the Bible and the classics, those two main sources of Western civilization, were the foundations upon which his theological training rested. Württemberg was the stronghold of German humanism. Tübingen University, and more particularly its Theological Seminary, were celebrated as centres of religious and classical scholarship. The great humanist Philipp Melanchthon, Luther's friend and the translator of Plato's *Symposium,* had taught at the Seminary. Johann Reuchlin had held the chair of Greek and Hebrew in the University. Among Hölderlin's own teachers there were classical scholars of high repute.

Württemberg at that thime was not merely the home of humanism in Germany but a centre of pietism as well. The pietists formed the most influential Protestant sect in the country. The reformer and pietist mystic Albrecht Bengel was responsible for disseminating a messianic movement throughout Swabia. In his

9

books, *Erklärte Offenbarung St Johannis* and *Ordo temporum a principio per periodus oeconomiae divinae historicas atque propheticas ad finem,* written in the first half of the eighteenth century, he had prophesied the imminent return of Christ. The influence of his teaching upon the Monastery Schools was considerable. The great majority of Swabian pietist poets came from these schools, especially from the Tübingen Seminary. The pietist church hymnal, in use when Hölderlin was a student, was written in the main by former pupils of the Seminary. A copy of Bengel's mystical commentary on the New Testament was among the books found in Hölderlin's library.

It was at Tübingen Seminary, on the inner gate of which were inscribed the words *Aedes Deo et Musis sacrae,* that Hölderlin studied Isaiah and Hesiod, the Gospels and Plato. Here, too, he composed sermons and translated from Homer and Lucan. An essay entitled *Die Parallele zwischen Salomons Sprichwörtern und Hesiods Werken und Tagen,* which he wrote as a student, lays stress upon the similarities between the two traditions. Solomon and Hesiod, Isaiah and Plato, the writers of the Gospels and the Greek tragedies, the psalmists and Homer, all these were to Hölderlin embodiments of a single ideal, the ideal of divine inspiration; and he had one ambition only, to join their ranks.

Hölderlin, like most of his contemporaries, was influenced as much by the heirs of the Graeco-Judaic tradition as by the ancients themselves, for it was not strictly from biblical or classical sources that his conception of the poet-prophet was derived. No such idea is to be found in the Bible itself. The Hebrew prophets did not look upon themselves as poets, nor were they so regarded by their people. The need of the hour brought them into being to direct the life of the nation and call the people to action. In ancient Greece, it is true, the poets expounded theology and interpreted myth, but the fact that Plato could denounce them as irreligious indicates that their position was by no means unassailable. Moreover, the Greek poet was not the only interpreter of Greek religion; there were also the seer (the *mantis,* called *vates* by the Romans) and the poet-philosopher such as Empedocles and Plato. It was not until the Renaissance that the poet-*vates,* entrusted with a prophetic message, a compound of Hebrew prophet, Greek poet, seer and philosopher-poet, found general acceptance as the poetic ideal.

In the twenty-fifth Canto of the *Paradiso* Dante expresses the hope that, on his return home, he may be crowned with the sacred laurel of Apollo in the very chapel in which he was baptised. This passage is symbolic both of the fusion of Christian and classical tradition in the work of Dante and of his belief that the life of the poet was one of religious dedication. It was Dante's admirer, Boccaccio, who summed up the poetic theory of his age. In the fourteenth and fifteenth books of his *Genealogia Deorum* he speaks of the divine origin of poetry. In this work the poets of ancient Greece are described as being directly inspired by the Holy Ghost and compared to Moses, David and Job. The following century, which rediscovered Plato's *Phaedrus* and *Ion*, found in these dialogues of the Greek philosopher a confirmation of Boccaccio's views. Plato's description of the divine madness which the Muses instil into the soul of the poet seemed to them the Greek equivalent of the doctrine of inspiration by the Holy Ghost. The typically Renaissance view of the *poeta theologus* or *sacer vates* found its way into German literature mainly through Opitz, the seventeenth century eclectic, who was influenced by the Italian, French and English theorists of the previous century. In the eighteenth century Klopstock and Herder carried it a stage further, and through their work it came down to Hölderlin. Hölderlin was himself one of the poets who embodied the Renaissance ideal. His spiritual forbears were Vida, Tasso, Ronsard and Sidney, as well as Milton and Klopstock. All these poets belong to the period which began with the Renaissance and ended some time after the French Revolution. The guiding spirit of this great era was the zeal for reform. I was a time of revolution, in the spheres of religion, national consciousness, and the social order, and the poet was swept along by these revolutions. In this world of changing values he was intensely conscious of his mission: the re-interpretation of Christian and classical ideals in the light of his own age. He felt himself to be the guardian of the past and the herald of the future, a worthy successor to the *vates* and the prophets.

Intimately associated with the reforming zeal of the Renaissance was a longing for the spiritual regeneration of the human soul. This longing found expression in the dissemination of mystical ideals which began at the close of the Middle Ages and continued without interruption into the eighteenth century. Its great importance for literature and the arts lay in its emphasis on the inward spiritual experience of the individual as the source of divine revelation. For the mystic the soul is a mirror which reflects God's love; he believes that it has been created because God needs the love of man almost as much as man needs the love of God. This is how a seventeenth-century German mystic, known as Angelus Silesius, expressed it:

11

Ich trage Gottes Bild: wenn Er sich will besehn
So kann es nur in mir und wer mir gleicht geschehn.

Gott ist in mir das Feuer, und ich in Ihm der Schein:
Sind wir einander nicht ganz inniglich gemein?

This idea was translated into the language of metaphysics by
Leibniz. Leibniz calls the human soul a 'little god', and, using
the familiar metaphor, describes it as a 'living mirror' not only
capable of reflecting the works of God, but itself endowed with
creative force (*Principes de la nature et de la grâce*). The symbol
of the mirror recurs in Schiller's poem *Die Freundschaft,* in the
original mystical sense:

> Freundlos war der grosse Weltenmeister,
> Fühlte Mangel – darum schuf er Geister,
> Sel'ge Spiegel seiner Seligkeit.

This concept plays a significant part in Hölderlin's later poetry.
There it is applied specifically to the poet, who appears as the
helpmate of the gods. Hölderlin was profoundly influenced by
mystical ideas, which came to him not only by way of Leibniz
and the early works of Schiller, but more directly through the
influence of Württemberg pietism. Pietism, which combined the
cult of inwardness with a messianic ideal, forms an essential
background to his poetry.

Hölderlin's century, while cherishing Christian ideas and
Christian ways of feeling, was yet no longer dominated by the
Christian Church. Its religious impulses were more and more
directed into secular channels, finding their fullest expression in
philosophy and art, which now had a new function—to re-interpret
life. The philosophers themselves began to stress the great significance of art. Pantheism in particular exerted a considerable
influence on eighteenth-century aesthetic theory. In his student
days Hölderlin came under this influence. He read Hemsterhuys,
Herder, Schiller's *Philosophische Briefe,* and F. H. Jakobi's
*Über die Lehre des Spinoza in Briefen an Herrn Moses Mendels-
sohn,* from which he copied extracts. Through this work he
became acquainted with the theories of Giordano Bruno, who defined God as the artist fashioning the world from within, and man
not as God's creature, but as part of the creative cosmic force
itself. In other words, God appears in the guise of the supreme
creative artist, and it follows that his imitator, the human artist,
takes on the character of a miniature god.

The eighteenth-century thinkers stressed the anthropocentric rather than the mystical implications of this idea, and worshipped at the shrine of genius. Shaftesbury's description of the poet as 'a second maker: a just Prometheus under Jove' found more than one echo in the literature and philosophy of the period, and added to the concepts of the poet as *vates,* mystic and artist that of the poet as a 'just' Titan.

In the view of some of Hölderlin's contemporaries, no artist had a greater claim than the poet to the title of creator, for his medium was language, through which God Himself ordained the Creation and revealed Himself to man. Herder in *Vom Geist der ebräischen Poesie* clearly indicates this function of the aesthetic tenets of the period with the Christian doctrine of *Logos.* Man, the 'visible god on earth', he says, 'by naming all things and thus, as a sentient being, relating all things to himself' becomes the imitator of the 'creating, naming (nennende) Godhead'.

Thus Hölderlin's vision of the ideal poet was compounded of diverse elements. The great figures of biblical and classical antiquity, the poet-*vates* of modern times, the chain of historical movements stretching from the Renaissance to the French Revolution, the newly emerged artist, secular successor to the mystic–all these combined to set Hölderlin upon the *holy way* of the poet.

III

Early Poems

In his autobiography Magenau, one of Hölderlin's friends at Tübingen, sets the scene for Hölderlin's early poems. Magenau, Neuffer and Hölderlin formed a poetry club which met once a week. At these sessions each member had to recite a poem. If the poem met with the approval of the others it was entered in a special book. Magenau tells us:

> We held one of these little parties on a most brilliant day in a pretty summer-house in the garden of the Lamb Inn. We were well supplied with Rhine wine, and we sang our way through all the Songs of Joy in succession. Schiller's Song of Joy we had reserved for the punch bowl . . . the bowl stood steaming on the table and we were about to begin the song when Hölderlin begged us first to cleanse ourselves of all our sins in the Castalian Spring. Near the garden flowed the so-called Philosopher's Fountain; that was Hölderlin's Castalian

Spring. We made our way there through the garden and washed our faces and hands. Neuffer was very solemn as he strode along: 'This song of Schiller's' said Hölderlin, 'no-one impure may sing!' Now we sang. At the stanza 'This glass to the Good Spirit' shining tears came into Hölderlin's eyes; full of enthusiasm he held his glass out of the window and roared: 'This glass to the Good Spirit' into the open air, so that the whole Neckar valley re-echoed.

The scenery of the lovely Neckar valley–a German Arcadia to those young lovers of the Muses–the delicious Rhine wine, a very happy and very earnest circle of academic friends,–what wonder that they overflowed with feeling as they burst into Shiller's rousing 'Seid umschlungen Millionen'. If we feel inclined to smile at the youthful and 'German' romanticism of it all, we must remember that similar groups of young people, roused to equal exuberance, could be found in many European countries at that time. We must fancy ourselves back in the age of which Wordsworth sang:

> Bliss was it in that dawn to be alive
> But to be young was very Heaven!

Those youths did not merely indulge in fanciful dreams, but, as the poet went on to say,

> Were called upon to exercise their skill,
> Not in Utopia–subterranean fields–
> Or some secreted island, Heaven knows where!
> But in the very world, which is the world
> Of all of us . . .

The great ideals of the century–liberty, equality and fraternity–seemed no longer ideals but living realities in those early days of the French Revolution.

It seemed then as though Rousseau's vision of natural man reborn in a new society was about to be fulfilled, and that all events conspired to vindicate Kant's belief in the autonomy of human reason. When Hölderlin, Neuffer and Magenau met to recite poetry it was not for the sake of mere aesthetic enjoyment, but because they felt themselves contributing to a great political and spiritual cause. Poetry for them, as for their beloved master Klopstock, was to be the basis of a new German national culture. Their friendship, modelled on that of Schiller's Don Carlos and

14

Marquis Posa, was to be the nucleus of a new society. They were full of exuberant optimism for the future. In 1793 Hölderlin wrote to his brother: 'I love the generations of centuries still to come . . . We are living in an age when everything is leading up to better times.' He and the two most famous of his Tübingen friends, Hegel and Schelling, joined a secret political society. Rumour had it that one day all three were found dancing round a Tree of Liberty, until it was brought home to them that such behaviour was not considered appropriate in the Duchy of Württemberg.

These young Swabians were in revolt not only against political tyranny, but against the dry dogmatism of theological teaching at the Seminary. For them, all the events of the time were illuminated and transformed by the eschatological ideals which had been spread abroad by Albrecht Bengel and his followers. The second coming of the Messiah and the return of the Golden Age were virtually the same thing in the eyes of these young men: they regarded the French Revolution as an important step towards the establishment of the Earthly Paradise; the 'Kingdom of God' and the 'ἓν καὶ πᾶν' were their watchwords.

Hegel during this time was working on his essay *Volksreligion*, in which he pointed out to his contemporaries that in ancient Greece and early Christendom religion had been the mainspring of community life. At the same time Schelling was writing on myths and legends as the sources of ancient culture. Hölderlin in his dissertation *Die Geschichte der schönen Künste unter den Griechen* showed how the Greeks drew their religious inspiration from the poets. Poetry, whose very heart was religion, was, he believed—echoing Herder—the supreme expression of a civilisation. He saw history past and present as a single long chain of divine manifestations, with the psalmists, Pindar, Plato and Klopstock as their interpreters. Hölderlin named all these in one breath as brothers in the 'abiding community of great minds'. His was no merely romantic nostalgia for Greece; he believed in the timeless example of antiquity. The past, for him, lived on, side by side with the present, for past, present and future are fused in an unbroken continuum. In the same spirit, and with affectionate familiarity, he called the Greek philosopher 'Mein Plato' and the author of *Night Thoughts* 'Mein Young'. Thus one stream of divine revelation, and one only, runs through the whole of history. At times it flows sluggishly, at others it rushes forward like a torrent.

At his period Hölderlin believed himself to be living through an age when the stream of divine revelation was in full spate,

15

flowing more powerfully than ever before since the days of Plato's Athens. His generation had set itself no less ambitious a task than the realization of all the highest and most venerable aspirations of mankind. The prophesies of ancient times, they believed, were at last on the verge of fulfilment. Hölderlin was exalted with the sense of a sacred mission. He would join the ranks of his great predecessors and contemporaries, and stand before all the world as the poet-prophet with a divinely inspired message to deliver. It was in this spirit that Hölderlin's first hymn-cycle was conceived.

The Tübingen hymns are born of a communal religious experience. This determines their character, themes, and diction. They are essentially hymns addressed to a community, not songs composed for individual readers. They are not concerned with the poet's personal moods, but affirm beliefs shared by the majority of his contemporaries. Their themes are love, friendship, freedom, destiny, and the harmony of the universe. In nearly all of them a goddess appears to teach the poet what he is to say. In his choice of metre and vocabulary, Hölderlin showed little originality; in the main he modelled himself upon Schiller. In fact, he did not set much store by originality. In a draft preface to his novel *Hyperion* he says: 'I have no wish that it should be original. Originality means novelty, but the things that are most dear to me are those that are as old as the world'. His imagery, too, is traditional. There are few traces in his early work of that personal feeling for nature which Rousseau brought into fashion. In the Tübingen hymns there is scarcely a mention of nature for its own sake, or for sake of the human emotions it aroused. Nature to him was part of a vast spiritual whole. In the natural order, to which all things, animate and inanimate, are subject, there is one guiding principle, the spirit of love:

> Ausgegossen ist des Lebens Schale,
> Bächlein, Sonnen treten in die Bahn,
> Liebetrunken schmiegen junge Tale
> Sich den liebetrunknen Hügeln an:

An earlier example shows clearly whence Hölderlin's vision of nature was derived:

> Was bist du Erde? hadert der Ozean,
> Was bist du? streck' ich nicht, wie die Fittiche
> Auf's Reh der Adler, meine Arme
> Ueber die Schwächliche aus?

16

Hölderlin's source was the Bible; for him nature meant the Creation. Even in later life, when his outlook had become more pantheistic than Christian, he still regarded nature as a complex of forces, each charged with ethos and emotion which testify as one to the grandeur of a divine spirit. In this vision lies what has been called the mythical quality of his poetry. Hence Hölderlin draws freely upon the rich symbolism of the past. Among his favourite recurrent images as the eagle signifying courage, the river signifying the eternal and heroic flow of life, the mountain signifying pride and freedom, the valley signifying humility. In the early hymns, Hölderlin more often than not used his symbols allegorically, as personified abstractions which he borrowed from Schiller. Schiller's allegories themselves are no more than late and somewhat petrified survivals of that wealth of living symbols which still flourish in Klopstock's odes, and which have their roots in the rich soil of Christian and humanists tradition. From this heritage Hölderlin derived his concepts and his language. Later, as his personality developed, his imagery became wider and deeper. In his mature poetry, there are no more allegories in the Schiller manner. This is not to say that he created new symbols, but that his genius infused new life into the traditional material which, when he first turned to it, seemed to have set into the ridigity of a convention. At all times his poetry springs from an ancient and universally accepted tradition.

This, however, is only one side of the picture. Hölderlin is not only the guardian of the past but also a very individual modern poet. His pure voice always rises like a solo above the choruses of tradition. He is most himself when he speaks of suffering and of joy. His capacity for joy and for that kind of suffering which springs from the privation of joy was the deepest element in his nature. When he said, in a letter written while he was still at school, that he was incapable of such happiness as his companions enjoyed, this was only true in the sense that, being intuitively aware of the nature of ecstasy, he could not be satisfied with anything less than the sublime. Throughout his life Hölderlin, with unusual simplicity and tenacity, preserved the dream of childhood. No experience, however shattering, could rob him of the innate certainty that it was possible for man to attain a state of infinite beatitude. The striving towards this state, the desire to lose himself in it, provides the great personal theme of all Hölderlin's poetry. This ideal of absolute joy is at once the dream of the child and the goal of the mystic. Hölderlin was a mystic in his passionate desire to embrace the absolute, to be united with it, to absorb it through all his senses. He longed to

17

get drunk on immortality. This state of intoxication is repeated over and over again in the Tübingen hymns. Yet there is no trace of sensuousness in these hymns, for the state they describe is one in which the body is overpowered by the soul. They are the expression of Hölderlin's intense spirituality. His is a 'furious yearning' for the absolute. It seizes him:

> Wie den Aar in grauem Felsenhange
> Wildes Sehnen nach der Sterne Bahn.

It is a fierce but 'sacred enthusiasm'. The poet feels his heart to be a flower on the immortal tree of God (*Das Schicksal*).

Yet Hölderlin is not in the fullest sense a mystic; he is a poet, and, being a poet, he stops short of the mystic's goal. He does not, like the mystic, surrender himself entirely to the divine, but turns back to his own heart and takes delight in savouring his experience. He glories in the enjoyment of intense religious emotion. He is filled with wonder at the 'heaven of the heart' which is capable of such ecstasies. The heart to him is not so much the seat of sensibility, sentiment and recollection as the source of the *one* instinct that matters: the instinct to follow blindly its native call and soar towards the celestial regions. These aspirations are indeed ambitious; yet, at the same time, Hölderlin was imbued throughout his life with the humility of the truly religious man. The clash between a boundless striving of the spirit and a true humility of the soul provides the dominant note of Hölderlin's character, and gives his later poetry its unmistakable tone and particular poignancy.

Hölderlin's personal aspirations are reflected in his picture of the ideal poet as well as in the language of his poetry. He sees the poet as a great, lonely, heroic figure, seeking self-perfection. He frequently compares him to Hercules and Achilles, and calls him the brother of heroes. Both the poet and the hero are conceived as superhuman figures, exposed to greater joy and sorrow than the rest of mankind. They are semi-mystics and Titans who stand in personal communion with God. To use Hölderlin's favourite symbols, they are like the eagle leaving his nest and soaring up into the skies, or the river rushing headlong towards the ocean. The eagle and the river are, as has been said, traditional symbols, but Hölderlin's love for them is significant. Both suggest the heroic impulse ceaselessly driving its subject upwards or onwards towards the very source of the divine power. Hölderlin's metre and style, like his ideas and imagery, are derivative yet peculiar to himself. In these early poems the metre and syntax are borrowed from Schiller, but the impassioned cadences and exalted climaxes spring from his own artless enthusiasm.

There is, however, one thing lacking in the Tübingen poems and their author–direct experience. Hölderlin, at this stage, is too ready to take wing without plumbing the depths of human experience. His emotion is disproportionate to the reality which touches it off, and this shows itself in an imperfect interpenetration of content and form. As in Schiller's poetry, the metrical and syntactical structure of the hymns seems like a garment detachable from the body of the poem. The reader is left with an impression of potential strength marred by immaturity.

Some of these poems, however, have a charm of their own. In them the youthful impetuousness of Hölderlin's faith is blended with an equally youthful tenderness and grace. These are the qualities to be found in the following stanzas of *Der Gott der Jugend* which he composed at the end of the Tübingen period. In them he is casting a backward glance at the bygone days of youth. As we listen to this personal incantation we can hear through it the echo of centuries of European tradition:

> Wie unter Tiburs Bäumen,
> Wenn da der Dichter sass,
> Und unter Götterträumen
> Der Jahre Flucht vergass,
> Wenn ihn die Ulme kühlte,
> Und wenn sie stolz und froh
> Um Silberblüten spielte,
> Die Flut des Anio;
>
> Und wie in Platons Hallen,
> Wenn durch der Haine Grün,
> Begrüsst von Nachtigallen,
> Der Stern der Liebe schien,
> Wenn alle Lüfte schliefen,
> Und, sanft bewegt vom Schwan,
> Cephissus durch Oliven
> Und Myrtensträuche rann:
>
> So schön ist's noch hienieden!
> Auch unser Herz erfuhr
> Das Leben und den Frieden
> Der freundlichen Natur;
> Noch blüht des Himmels Schöne,
> Noch mischen brüderlich

In unsers Herzens Töne
Des Frühlings Laute sich.

Drum such' im stillsten Tale
Den düftereichsten Hain,
Und giess aus goldner Schale
Den frohen Opferwein!
Noch lächelt unveraltet
Das bild der Erde dir,
Der Gott der Jugend waltet
Noch über dir und mir.

IV

Encounters

On the recommendation of Schiller, Hölderlin obtained his first
post as house tutor to the son of Charlotte von Kalb in Waltershausen near Jena. He took up his appointment with a high sense
of responsibility, in the knowledge that his educational theories
were now to be put to the test. Conscientiously, he reported to
Schiller on the progress of his pupil, whom he was attempting to
mould in the likeness of Rousseau's Emile. But all his efforts were
wasted. The boy was dull and difficult, and he could make nothing of him. Worry and disappointment over his failure began to
endanger Hölderlin's delicate health. In the autumn of 1794 he
and his pupil left Waltershausen for Jena. Soon after this, Charlotte von Kalb released him from his employment. In recognition
of his services and talents, she provided him with the means of
pursuing his studies independently for some months to come.
Thus, after his first and unsuccessful attempt as a teacher, he
found himself a student again.

Jena, at that time, was the cultural centre of Germany. In that
brilliant milieu we can picture Hölderlin's tall, slender figure
moving shyly among some of the most famous men of his age.
Shortly before he arrived in Jena, Fichte had been appointed to
the chair of philosophy. Hölderlin attended his lectures and
greatly admired his fiery and 'titanic' personality. Earlier in the
year a meeting of the Jena Society of Natural Scientists had
brought together Goethe and Schiller and had marked the beginning of their friendship. Schiller lived in Jena, and Goethe
often came over from nearby Weimar to visit him. As editor of
the journal *Thalia* and the newly founded *Horen*, Schiller gath-

ered around him all the literary stars of Germany. He knew how
to attract young talent as well as men of established fame. Goethe,
Herder, W. von Humboldt, Körner, the young brothers Schlegel,
and occasionally Hölderlin himself, contributed to his period-
icals. It was the magnetism of Schiller's personality which had
drawn Hölderlin to Jena; he was overjoyed to be there, so close
to his master and protector. In a letter to Neuffer of November
1794, he gives a pathetic account of his first visit to Schiller's
house. In the drawing-room he was introduced to a man whose
name he did not catch. The stranger asked him some polite
questions, which he answered in an indifferent, absent-minded
manner, his whole attention being focussed on Schiller. That
same evening he discovered that the stranger had been Goethe.
Some time after he visited Weimar, and was received kindly by
both Goethe and Herder.

Goethe was susceptible to the naïve charm of Hölderlin's personality and of his early poems. His delightful comment on the
poem *An den Aether* which Schiller sent him for criticism, was
that 'one is reminded of those paintings in which all the animals
gather round Adam in Paradise'. (June 28th, 1797.) When in
1797 he saw Hölderlin in Frankfurt at Schiller's request, he
found him 'amiable, open-hearted and modest almost to the point
of timidity'. He added, pedantically, that 'he has appropriated a
fair number of your (Schiller's) best ideas quite successfully so
that he was able to grasp some topics with great ease'. (August
23rd, 1797.) This is the last time Hölderlin's name appeared in
the Schiller-Goethe correspondence. For Hölderlin, the Olym-
pian Goethe remained an awe-inspiring stranger.

But his reverence for Goethe and the Jena intellectuals was
nothing in comparison with his obsessional devotion to Schiller.
Hölderlin had idolised Schiller from boyhood. The rhythm of
Schiller's poems had imposed itself upon his youthful hymns, the
militant idealism of Schiller's early dramas had transported him
with rapture, and during his stay in Jena the man himself cast
his spell over him. To Schiller, Hölderlin was no more than a talented but rather helpless young fellow-Swabian, in whom he took
a friendly and detached interest. There was little affection on
Schiller's side, and not the faintest recognition of the younger
poet's remarkable promise. Hölderlin, though conscious of this
lack of real response, still clung to his friendship. At the same
time, he realised that his dependence on the master was arresting
his development, and he even made some attempt to break free,
but to no avail; he was not able to overcome his first childlike
adoration. Goethe, on one occasion, remarked that Schiller could

not help being great whatever he did—he was great 'even when he cut his finger nails'. (*Eckermann,* January 17th, 1827.) But there was also an element of ruthlessness in Schiller's greatness, of which Goethe was aware. Both these qualities were apparent in Schiller's relation with Hölderlin; but Hölderlin was so overwhelmed by the older man's greatness that he was blind to his ruthlessness. Years after he had left Jena he confessed to Schiller in a letter: 'Believe me . . . it is not possible for me to be near you. The truth is, you excite me too much, when I am with you. I still remember so well how your presence always used to inflame me, so that the whole of the next day I was unable to think. As long as I was with you I felt my heart shrivel up, and after I had left you it swelled almost past bearing. In your presence I am like a plant which has only just been put into the soil: it has to be sheltered at high noon.' (Frankfurt, August 1797.) Some years later, when he desperately needed help, he turned to Schiller, but his old friend had not even the grace to reply to his appeal. Of all Hölderlin's personal relationships, this was the most pathetic.

If Hölderlin felt awkward with the great men of Jena, he was just as much out of place in the intense intellectual climate of the town as a whole. At that time, Jena was the junction of the two great German cultural streams, philosophical idealism and literary classicism. Yet the community spirit to which Hölderlin had been accustomed in Tübingen was lacking in Jena. This was partly due to the political situation. Enthusiasm for the French Revolution gave way to disillusionment and anxiety as in France the Terror reached its peak. Many leading German writers either tried to avert their gaze altogether from the political scene or dealt with events by theorising. Their attitude was conditioned by political frustration in Germany itself. 'Where is Germany?' asked Goethe and Schiller in the *Xenien:*

> Deutschland wo liegt es? ich weiss das Land nicht zu finden,
> Wo das gelehrte beginnt, hört das politische auf.

It was not merely that there was no political *élan* but that there was no corporate religious faith to hold the country together.

In Jena, Hölderlin witnessed the belated German Renaissance. This, abortive as it was in its attempt at religious, social and national revivals, gave birth only to a great literary and philosophical movement initiated by a handful of men of genius, and appealing only to the chosen few. The leaders were well aware that their cultural gains had been bought at heavy cost. They knew that the bonds of a common faith, such as had given strength to earlier generations, had been, for them, irretrievably broken. Most of them suffered from a sense of isolation. No one had felt the pain of personal renunciation more keenly than the young author of *Die Leiden des jungen Werthers*; but Goethe made good his losses in the contemplation of nature and art. Schiller too, in his youth, had mourned the vanished gods, myths and metaphysics of past ages, and had summed up the position of the modern poet in the bitter words: 'und uns blieb das entseelte Wort'. While Hölderlin was in Jena, Schiller, although he never quite abandoned his own metaphysical aspirations, was under the spell of Kant's anti-metaphysical and moral philosophy. He was then occupied with his *Briefe über die aesthetische Erziehung des Menschen*, in which he attempt to reassess the relationship between aesthetic and moral values. Hölderlin eagerly absorbed everything Schiller wrote or told him, and incorporated some of his ideas in his theoretical essays. Yet, much as Schiller's emphasis on art as a means of education appealed to him, his own approach was different. For Hölderlin, the Kantian renunciation of metaphysics was not to be contemplated. He could not, and indeed would not, abandon his faith. Schiller's problem, the reconciliation of morality and art, was no problem to Hölderlin, for he quite simply believed that both were aspects of man's relations with the divinity.

His own beliefs, however, were challenged by the philosophy of Fichte. Hölderlin did feel drawn to the uncompromising idealism of Fichte, but in the long run he withstood the philosopher's influence. Indeed, he could not do otherwise, for there was that in his nature which was fundamentally opposed to the trend of Fichte's thought. As a poet for whom life was a dialogue with the divinity and who addressed the earth and the air as '*Du*, Mutter Erde' and '*Du*, Vater Aether', he could not accept a doctrine based on the proposition that there was no reality outside the Ego. For some time he wrestled with Fichte's philosophy, but though he expended a great deal of intellectual and emotional energy upon it, he gained little from it in the end. Thus everything combined to shake Hölderlin's self-confidence. He could not thrive in that atmosphere which so stimulated the lively band of romantics who came to settle in Jena a few years after his departure.

On the verge of a breakdown, without money, and discouraged by the insignificance of his achievements, Hölderlin left Jena in the summer of 1795 and returned home. Here he wrote the poem *An die Natur*, which is a sad counterpart to *Der Gott der Jugend*:

23

Tot ist nun, die mich erzog und stillte,
Tot ist nun die jugendliche Welt.

The very foundations of Hölderlin's faith seemed to crumble. His encounter with German philosophy did not end here, however. It so happened that while he was at home, and again a year later, he met his friend Schelling. The following year brought him together with Hegel, who had, like himself, accepted a tutorship in Frankfurt. Hegel, who later came to be regarded as the complacent Prussian State philosopher, was, at that time, a young man, deeply stirred by a vision of life, infinite and beyond the compass of reason. He was the autor of a mystical poem, *Eleusis,* which he wrote for Hölderlin in anticipation of their reunion, and in which he looks forward to

der Gewissheit Wonne,
Des alten Bundes Treue fester, reifer noch zu finden,
Des Bundes, den kein Eid besiegelte,
Der freien Wahrheit nur zu leben,
Frieden mit der Satzung,
Die Meinung und Empfindung regelt, nie, nie einzugehn.

Thus Hölderlin renewed contact with his Tübingen friends–the two men who were to become the leading German philosophers of their day. With them he felt at ease, and found himself once more in the company of men whose way of thought was congenial. The three friends indulged in a lively exchange of ideas, which has since caused much conjecture and controversy among literary historians. They, like Fichte and Schiller, were thoroughly at home with the dialectical mode of thought and feeling, and they shared that pantheistic vision of life which was rooted in Swabian mysticism and derived its idealistic bias from contemporary thought. Schelling believed in the identity of spirit (Geist) and nature, Hegel in that of spirit and history. Hölderlin's attitude was, in some sense, a synthesis of his friends', since he saw genius as the embodiment of the divine spirit which manifests itself both in nature and in history.

Fundamentally, of course, Hölderlin did not think in philosophical terms. It is in fact most interesting to note how, after having taken great pains to elaborate a philosophical concept, he suddenly translates it back into his own language of concrete experience. For him philosophy was above all a means to an end. At times he even want so far as to regard it as a distracting sideline. In a letter to Hegel he wrote: 'It is fortunate . . . that the

24

aerial spirits with metaphysical wings which accompanied me from Jena have left me since I came to Frankfurt.' (November 1796.)

The place of these spirits had in the meantime been usurped by a real human being, the person who was to be the most decisive influence in Hölderlin's life. Hölderlin had come to Frankfurt in December 1795, as tutor to the family of the rich banker Gontard. Gontard's wife Susette, a beautiful, cultured and noble woman, soon returned the love which the young tutor felt for her. To him she was Diotima, the priestess who in Plato's *Symposium* teaches Socrates the nature of true love. He, for the first and only time in his life, felt himself understood by a kindred spirit who shared all his joys and sorrows. She too, having had an unhappy married life, experienced for the first time the ecstacy of a complete communion of spirit. With love there came to each of them a sense of the presence of God. In Hölderlin's own words:

Aber wir, zufrieden gesellt, wie die liebenden Schwäne,
Wenn sie ruhen am See, oder, auf Wellen gewiegt,
Niedersehn in die Wasser, wo silberne Wolken sich spiegeln,
Und aetherisches Blau unter den Schiffenden wallt,
So auf Erden wandelten wir. Und drohte der Nord auch,
Er, der Liebenden Feind, klagenbereitend, und fiel,
Von den Ästen das Laub, und flog im Winde der Regen,
Ruhig lächelten wir, fühlten den eigenen Gott
Unter trautem Gespräch, in Einem Seelengesange,
Ganz in Frieden, mit uns kindlich und freudig allein.
Menons Klagen um Diotima

But this perfect peace was not to last. It was not long before the lovers found themselves the helpless victims of circumstance. Susette's husband insulted Hölderlin and he, conscious of his innocence, was deeply wounded. One day in September 1798, after un unpleasant scene with Gontard, Höderlin secretly left the house and fled to the small neighbouring town of Homburg. From there he and Susette exchanged letters and snatched secret meetings. Only a few drafts of Hölderlin's letters have been preserved, whereas Susette's have come down to us and are among the finest love letters in literature. After a time the lovers found the courage to part for good, so that the memory of their love might be preserved in all its strength and purity.

Once again Hölderlin was alone; but in the meantime he had found himself. Through his great love and great sorrow his genius had matured.

25

V

Hyperion

Much of Hölderlin's personal experience in Jena and in Frankfurt is reflected in *Hyperion*. In 1797 the first part of the final version was published, and was followed by the second part in 1799. *Hyperion* is one of those novels which, in tracing the development of an individual character, arrive at a philosophy of life. This genre was popular at the time; Wieland had introduced it into German literature in *Agathon*, and Goethe had brought it to perfection in *Wilhelm Meister*.

Wilhelm Meisters Lehrjahre appeared almost simultaneously with *Hyperion*. But apart from the genre, the two works have little in common. Unlike Goethe, Hölderlin does not treat the development of his hero as a process of progressive evolution. Hyperion's life is rather the revolution of a wheel than the forward drive of a plough, and his spiritual growth consists not in the steady enlargement of personality, but rather in the deepening of consciousness through a recurrent experience. Hölderlin achieves the effect of a timeless movement in time, and this impression is enhanced by the form of the novel: the story is told in retrospect, in a series of letters which Hyperion writes to a friend, in which the events of the past are interspersed with and related to the thoughts and feelings of the present. In contrast to Goethe, Hölderlin is not interested in human personality as such; he attempts little psychological analysis; his characters are not individuals in the sense in which Goethe's are. Hyperion, who takes his name from the Sun-god, is a symbolical figure; but even he is not important in himself; what matters is his relationship with the world outside. For him, life depends upon the fullest possible communication with men and God. His love for teacher, friend, mistress and community are the corner stones of a pyramid of which God is the apex. But in the end Hyperion's longing for communion is not fulfilled and he remains a lonely and solitary figure.

Indeed *Hyperion,* in both mood and form, is mere akin to Goethe's *Werther* than to *Wilhelm Meister,* for both stories are told in a series of letters and the keynote of both is loneliness. Yet, if we compare Hyperion's sense of loneliness with that of Werther, we find that they are different in kind. Hyperion, Werther's junior by almost twenty-five years, nevertheless gives the impression of being his elder brother. Werther's tragedy is more modern as well as more poignant and more complete.

It is true that in Hyperion's *Song of Destiny* no less than in Werther's letters we hear the 'voice of the moral, completely driven into himself, incomplete in himself and inexorably falling downwards', but, unlike Werther, Hyperion does not lose his faith that the gods are there, 'high up in the light', even if man is cast down into darkness. The seeds of perfection are to be found in human relations. He has known people who, if they could be united in a common effort, might bring into being the ideal community. Hyperion is a hermit, it is true, but, in the words of the sub-title a 'hermit in Greece'.

The scene of the novel is Greece in the year 1770 at a time when the Greeks were fighting against Turkey. We follow the young Hyperion in his wanderings through the rugged countryside of the Peloponnese, along the banks of the river Eurotas, across the valleys of Elis, Nemea and Olympia. We see him gazing up at the snowy peaks of Helicon and Parnassus from the Corinthian Isthmus, sailing across to the coasts of Ionia, exploring the neighbourhood of Smyrna, and following the river Caystros towards the mountain range of the Tmolus. Hölderlin acquired his knowledge of local geography largely from a German translation of the works of Richard Chandler, *Travels in Asia Minor* and *Travels in Greece*. Some of the picturesque details and the description of the naval battle were inspired by Choiseul-Gouffrier's *Voyage pittoresque de la Grèce*. But Hölderlin's vision of Greece is essentially his own. He saw it as a country of grace and grandeur with a thousand fragrant mountains 'rising incessantly up towards the sun one behind the other'. In his mind's eye, cataracts thunder down the rocks into the woods like young giants shouting with joy, while a light, at once tender and transparent, descends like a heavenly exhalation. While nature has remained the same, history has changed, and Hyperion is startled in his dreams by the 'cry of the jackal who sings his wild funeral dirge among the rubble-heaps of antiquity'.

Hyperion is not alone amid the ruins of his country. From time to time, he meets a spirit who, like himself, longs for the rebirth of his people. His first encounter is with Adamas, an almost legendary figure. Of him Hyperion says: 'his brow was laid bare to the morning stars and his eye penetrated the celestial spaces'. Adamas initiates his disciple in the secrets of history, and awakens in him the belief in man's godlike nature. One day, however, after a solemn farewell, he departs, and Hyperion is left behind in a mood of utter dejection. His second encounter is with Alabanda. 'We met like two rivers, tumbling down from the mountain, throwing off their load of earth and stone and rotten

27

wood and the whole chaotic sludge that impedes them, in order
to make a way towards each other'. The friends picture themselves as future companions-in-arms in a common fight against
tyranny and mediocrity. But so ecstatic is their relationship that
a single misunderstanding is enough to cause a sudden breach;
Alabanda had introduced his companion to a number of strange
men, members of the brotherhood of 'Nemesis', to whom Hyperion takes an instinctive dislike. He believes his friend to be in
secret sympathy with these men. Alabanda is too proud to defend
himself, and they part in bitterness and grief. Hyperion sinks
into an abyss of despair. Finally spring comes, and 'beetles and
swallows and pigeons and storks bustled about in joyous confusion, in the depths and in the heights, and things earthbound
took wing; the horses stormed over ditches, the deer over fences;
from the bottom of the sea the fish rose and skipped about on the
surface'. This is the overture to Hyperion's meeting with Diotima. For a while the narrative seems suspended like Diotima's
song itself, 'in golden mid-air between height and depth', while
Hyperion conjures up the times when 'out of one cup with the
beloved' he drank 'the delights of the world'. His love for her,
like that of Hölderlin for Susette, transcends personality. Like
Dante's Beatrice, Diotima embodies the poet's vision of the
divine. She becomes Hyperion's spiritual guide in his travels
through the wider world. Part I ends with a scene amid the ruins
of Athens, where Hyperion, encouraged by Diotima, decides to
go out and build the society of his dreams. He is to be the *vates*
and leader of his people.

In the second part we find Hyperion leading the Greeks to war
against Turkey. The political liberation of his country is the first
step towards the realisation of his plans. He is joined by Alabanda, but their common fight is doomed to failure. Their band of
soldiers betray the noble cause by pilfering, robbing and murder-
ing enemy and friend alike. Hyperion's hopes for the future are
completely shattered. From now on the story hastens to its inevitable, tragic end. The ideal community is not realised. In his
bitter disillusionment, Hyperion finds himself alone once more.
Alabanda leaves Hyperion and gives himself up to the men of
'Nemesis', to whom he had pledged himself in his youth. Diotima
dies. Hyperion seeks refuge amongst the Germans, but they too
are tainted with the sickness of the times. He breaks into a wild
condemnation of this nation: 'I cannot imagine a people more
dismembered than the Germans. You see artisans but no human
beings, priests but no human beings, masters and servants, young
and elderly people but no human beings–is this not like a battle-

field where hands and arms and limbs all lie scattered about while the life's blood is shed and ebbs away into the sand?' He returns to Greece, broken-hearted, finding consolation only in communion with nature.

The two parallel themes of this novel are the hero's relationship to the divinity and his attempt to build a new world. The celestial fields, which seemed within such easy reach in the early hymns, are, at times, inaccessible to Hyperion. There are moments when he doubts their very existence. 'O formerly, ye sinister brethren, it was otherwise', he exclaims, 'our hearts too rose triumphantly upwards and broke through the barrier, but as we looked, alas, there was an infinite void'. 'Es ist, als säh' ich, aber dann erschreck' ich wieder, als wär' es meine eigne Gestalt, was ich gesehn, es ist als fühlt' ich ihn, den Geist der Welt, aber ich erwache und meine, ich habe meine eignen Finger gehalten.' The nihilism of these remarks is the inseparable companion of modern egotism. Hölderlin had met with an extreme and metaphysical form of egotism in the philosophy of Fichte. Hyperion's despair, however, is not merely the outcome of a philosophical theory. It is the expression of a personal experience which Hölderlin himself must have been through. The experience arises out of a self-stultifying impulse. The soul's limitless desire for participation in the essence of divinity is unattainable, and in the very act of striving towards the unattainable the soul loses touch with God. It is the pseudo-mystical approach to the divine which recurs throughout Hölderlin's later works. Hyperion's feelings of doubt and guilt are the outcome of this disturbing relationship.

The dominant note, however, as far as the hero's personal religion is concerned, is one of confidence. Hyperion's one source of consolation is nature. The biblical concept of nature as Creation is still present in this novel, and the language and rhythms of the Bible, the Psalms and Lamentations, are echoed in the cadences of its prose. But overshadowing the biblical view of nature is Hyperion's pantheistic vision of a world peopled with divine shapes. These gods bear no resemblance to the allegorical goddesses of freedom, truth and harmony which appeared in the Tübingen hymns. The nature gods of *Hyperion*, indeed, all the gods of Hölderlin's poetry from now on, are incarnations of divine life. It is of these gods that Hölderlin says:

> Nur ihr, mit eurer ewigen Jugend, nährt
> In Herzen, die euch lieben, den Kindersinn,
> Und lasst in Sorgen und in Irren
> Nimmer den Genius sich vertrauern.

29

Of all these gods, the one who best exemplifies Hölderlin's ideal is the 'enchanting' Sun-Youth-God, the divine prototype of his hero Hyperion. It is this god who, in the poem *Sonnenuntergang*, plays 'with abundant golden chords on a divine lyre his song of evening'.

There is an elemental quality about Hölderlin's gods. In that they are outside the sphere of good and evil, they are pagan figures; yet at the same time, in their delicacy and humility, they bear a family relationship to Fra Angelico's angels. They all seem to breathe the air of the early Renaissance. Hyperion is reminiscent of St Francis of Assisi addressing sun, stars, water and earth as his brothers and sisters. For him, too, all the elements and phenomena of nature are members of one family. There is, however, a significant difference between the two. Whereas St Francis in his *Hymn to the Sun* acknowledges a hierarchy in the Creation, Hyperion recognises no such over all pattern; for he perceives the world not so much in relation to the Lord of Creation as to the heart of man. All nature seems to bear the impress of his own heart. All created things are thus drawn together in a close bond of intimacy. 'Like flowers from the dark earth' stars spring forth 'from the womb of night'; the valley is filled with warm light; 'joyous beams of sunlight' fall down 'like a rain of blossom'; thawing little clouds 'creep over the meadow like dreams', and stars blissfully peep through the branches like watchful genii. It is with the eyes of a loving child that Hyperion looks at the world, and the world reflects his loving gaze. 'Heaven of the night . . . thou art vaulted above me like a vine-clad bower, and like grapes thy stars hang down in clusters.'

For Hyperion the human heart is the symbol of life. The pulsations of the heart, the blood which pours into it and gushes out of it, represent for him the principle which governs all existence. 'Like the dissensions of lovers are the discords of the world. In the midst of strife is reconciliation, and all that is divided is re-united. The arteries of the heart part and meet again, and all is one eternal, glowing life.' These words, which reveal the neo-platonic and mystical origin of the thought, express the essence of Hyperion's experience. They recall Diotima's vision of human life, 'through change we manifest perfection, we divide the great harmonies of joy into varied melodies', and Hyperion's definition of beauty, based on a quotation from Heraclitus, as the 'One which is divided in itself'. Beauty, Nature, Greece, Love, and Diotima are different manifestations (and, on some levels, interchangeable symbols) of the same law of existence. This law can also be described as rhythm, a term which Hölderlin uses often in his philosophical prose essays. The principle of rhythm determines both the form and content of the novel: the letters written in retrospect with their rhythmic interchange of past and present, the rise and fall of the sentences, and the moods, the cycle of the seasons, of birth and decay, the meeting and parting of characters, and the coming and going of divine presences. Insight into the rhythm of life is, according to Hyperion, the beginning and end of philosophy. Piously and devoutly, he learns to accept the ebb and flow of life, of joy and sorrow. Thus the sacred principle of·unity is realised through the polarisation and magnetism of opposites. As a poet Hyperion delights in the 'Lebenslied der Welt', in which every discord is but part of a greater harmony. For him art, which brings every individual experience into relation with the whole of life, is the supreme expression of reality.

Hyperion, however, does not merely seek personal consolation. He is the bearer of a message to his people. His aim is to build a new society. For Hölderlin the metaphysical and the social issues are inseparable. Adamas, Alabanda and Diotima are as much members of the ideal community of the future as they are manifestations of the divine spirit. Greece is both a timeless symbol and a real country which must be liberated. Nature· to him is at once the holy abode of the gods and the treasure of a new social order. Even Beauty is not merely an aesthetic conception, it is a principle to be striven after in social life; he speaks of a 'theocracy of Beauty'. As a pietist, he longs for the 'new Church, the favourite child of the times'. Hölderlin in *Hyperion* indicates two possible courses for the realisation of a new society. One is that of the brotherhood of 'Nemesis', the other is that of Hyperion and his friends.

The 'Bund der Nemesis' is of special historical significance. Here is one of the few instances of a German writer coming to grips with the French Revolution. The 'Bund' stands for the terrorism and moral and political dictatorship of the Revolution. Its members, somewhat reminiscent of Schiller's *Räuber*, are fanatical and misguided idealists who believe that the ends justify the means. They symbolise the inhumanity of the law which, Hölderlin believes, has 'corrupted the bonds of love and made fetters of them' (*Der Rhein*). They also personify religious dogmatism, against which Hölderlin revolted in early youth. Hyperion recoils from them in horror, and escapes from their presence at the first opportunity.

The course chosen by Hyperion is diametrically opposed to that advocated by the men of 'Nemesis'. He believes in the 'divine right of the heart'. His views are a blend of mystical ideas and the social tenets of Rousseau. 'Holy nature, thou art the same within me and without. It cannot be so difficult to unite the divine life within to the world outside'. So he believes, but he is soon disillusioned. His political efforts fail completely. In the end Hyperion gives up all hope of improving men, and retires into solitude. The novel suggests that the responsibility for his failure rests almost entirely with society. The masses are devoid of noble feeling; they do not want to be educated; they are completely soulless. The cause of Hyperion's frustration is the godlessness of the age. Yet the reader feels that the tragic conclusion is not due only to the harshness of the world, but also to a weakness in the hero. Hyperion is not the man to set his country in order. He has little knowledge of men. As Diotima rightly divines, he is not concerned fundamentally with human beings, but with gods. The man who stands in constant need of divine reassurance is lacking in the qualities of the political leader. Hyperion is unable to come to grips with life. He is, like Shelley in Matthew Arnold's portrait, 'a beautiful and ineffectual angel beating in the void his luminous wings in vain'.

At the end of the novel we find on the one hand a dehumanised society, and on the other the solitary individual abandoning himself to a private communion with nature. Both states are products of the contemporary situation as it appeared to Hölderlin. Though Hölderlin believed that ideally the corporate life of society and the inner life of the individual were one, he saw and lamented the impassable gulf which, in the circumstances of his own day, divided them. Hyperion is the story of an attempt to bridge this gulf by love and faith, and as such, and in its simple and touching sincerity, it is a work of lasting value.

VI

Empedokles

The legend of the death of Empedokles on Mount Etna kindled Hölderlin's imagination while he was still working on *Hyperion*. It appeared to him a suitable subject for tragedy. In 1797 he sketched a plan for a drama called *Der Tod des Empedokles*. During the following years he wrote three fragmentary versions of the play and one prose essay in which he tried to clarify his ideas on the subject. Of all these the most valuable artistically is the third attempt at the play entitled *Empedokles auf dem*

Aetna, composed about 1800. The most nearly complete, however, is the first version of *Der Tod des Empedokles,* and for this reason it provides the best material for a critical analysis.

Hölderlin's Empedokles is an interesting and complex character. His principal source for the work was Diogenes Laertius's *De vitis, dogmatibus et apophthegmatibus clariorum philosphorum.* At the same time his hero is the favourite child of his own imagination. Empedokles, poet, magician, prophet, political reformer and saviour of his people, exemplifies the genius as Hölderlin imagined him. All those ideas which had fused in his mind to form his conception of the poet are apparent in Empedokles.

To begin with the contemporary views, Empedokles is a disciple of Rousseau. He stands for the political ideals of this modern writer, and is possessed by a most un-Greek longing for nature. At the same time he represents in the highest degree that human self-consciousness and reason characteristic of a contemporary of Kant's. According to the prose essay, he has also to fulfil the mission ascribed by Schiller to the artist: he has to mediate between the realms of nature and art. His place in history is seen from a Hegelian point of view: he is one of those great figures who emerge in times of crisis to resolve the conflict of their age. Finally Empedokles can be compared to Goethe's Faust in his desire to embrace the whole of existence in one glorious moment. He, like Faust, is the epitome of genius.

This complex of ideals can be traced back ultimately to a single source—mysticism. This mystical core is always apparent in Hölderlin. His Empedokles, the son of Nature and Reason, is essentially the man in whom the 'unio mystica' between the divine and the human is achieved. In him the souls of mortals and gods merge into a single essence. He says of himself:

> Geselle das Fremde, . . . denn ich
> Das Unbekannte nennet mein Wort,
> Und die Liebe der Lebenden trag'
> Ich auf und nieder; was einem gebricht,
> Ich bring es vom andern, und binde
> Beseelend, und wandle
> Verjüngend die zögernde Welt.

It is characteristic of Hölderlin that, in these lines, one of the main functions of the intermediary is the right use of language. By naming what had hitherto been nameless und unknown, he creates a new link between gods and men. His word is a rejuvenating as well as a binding force. He achieves, in the true sense of

33

the word, a new *religio*. Since it is the business of the poet to set a standard in the use of words, he must be regarded as the guardian of religion. These ideas recall Herder's philosophy of language, while the image of the shuttle movement of cosmic forces goes back to neo-platonic sources.

Empedokles, however, is more than a poet and an intermediary. He is the saviour who lays down his life for his people. Both in his mission and his fate he reminds us of Christ. The references to bread and wine and to the thunderstorm before his death are clearly allusions to the Gospels. However, when Empedokles asks his disciples the question: 'But who sayest thou that I am?' ('Wofür erkennst du mich?'), Pausanias answers: 'O son of Uranus'; and we then see Hölderlin's saviour in the guise of a Greek demi-god. His ancesters are Prometheus, Tantalus and Œdipus, the suffering heroes of ancient Greece. Above all he is the Greek philosopher and statesman Empedocles, who lived in the Sicilian town of Agrigentum in the fifth century B.C., and who believed that the world was governed by the opposing principles of love and hatred.

Like the historical Empedocles, the hero of Hölderlin's play comes into conflict with the citizens of his town. These are represented by the archon, Kritias, and the priest Hermokrates. These two accuse Empedokles of blasphemy, incite the people against him, and succeed in hounding him into exile. The Hermokrates of the first version has much in common with the men of 'Nemesis' in *Hyperion*. As the mouthpiece of state religion and dogma he is the arch enemy of genius. In the second version the priest appears in a milder aspect, and in *Empedokles auf dem Aetna,* he has changed into the wise Egyptian, Manes, who ranges himself on the side of tradition against the revolutionary spirit of genius. A parallel development, from the hatred of established institutions to a measure of reverence for them, can be traced in the later poems. Nevertheless, for Hölderlin divinely inspired genius always stands above and beyond Church and State.

In this drama the conflict between Empedokles and the people is the outcome of his inner conflict with the gods. This inner conflict goes back to a passage in Diogenes Laertius, where it is said that Empedocles boasted of being divine. This boast Hölderlin interprets not as a revolt against the gods but, characteristically, as a result of too intense a love for them. Empedokles's crime is one of which only genius is capable. In a moment of religious fervour Empedokles has felt himself to be one with the divine and, in a state of ecstasy, has declared himself a god. His sin is an expression of that pseudo-mystical experience previously met with in *Hyperion*. Hölderlin compares it to the *hubris* of the Greek Titans, and in the second version gives it added dramatic force by using the Prometheus myth. This *hubris* Hölderlin relates to the overweening pride of his own age, the age of enlightenment, in making his hero exclaim in a mood of bitter irony:

> . . . zur Magd ist mir
> Die herrnbedürftige Natur geworden,
> Und hat sie Ehre noch, so ist's von mir.
> Was wäre denn der Himmel und das Meer
> Und Inseln und Gestirn und was vor Augen
> Den Menschen alles liegt, was wär' es auch
> Dies tote Saitenspiel, gäb' ich ihm Ton
> Und Sprach' und Seele nicht? was sind
> Die Götter und ihr Geist, wenn ich sie nicht
> Verkündige!

This criticism of contemporary life embraces self-criticism. The sin of Empedokles, like his mission, is related to the poet's particular problem, that of language. Empedokles has abused the gift of language by proclaiming his unity with the gods, and in so doing has divulged a divine secret. As the priest says, he has 'laid bare his soul' and has 'talked away the god'. Human speech is governed by the 'sacred laws of seemliness', and Empedokles has overreached himself by transgressing against these laws. Language, according to Hölderlin, has two functions which are at once contradictory and complementary. At times it must be used to clothe ideas in 'holy sobriety', at others to strip them naked. Hölderlin believed that only true humility could teach the poet to use the gift of speech in the right way at the right moment. Empedokles has failed in this, and his punishment is that he is to be the mouthpiece of the gods no longer. Exile from their company is torment greater than he can bear:

> Allein zu sein und ohne Götter, ist der Tod.

Driven out by his people, and alone but for his faithful disciple, he starts on his way to Mount Etna.

The second part of the drama portrays genius reconciled to men and gods in the shadow of death. As Empedokles approaches Mount Etna the citizens of his town, having repented of their verdict, come to recall him and to make him their king. Empedokles refuses their offer with indignation, and tells them that he is determined to die. Now the hour has come for him to deliver

35

his great message. It is the gospel of re-birth, of the regeneration of man and society. In his vision Empedokles sees his age as a decaying body from which a young, rebellious spirit is struggling to free itself, so that it may emerge into the light of the world like a new-born child. The people must put the past behind them, and learn anew the lessons of love and piety. Then and then only a new era will dawn. Men will come face to face once more with the living gods, and the spirits of man and immortal will rejoice together in their reunion.

These are the last words of the *vates* to the world. From now on his death acquires a new meaning. He, who has been the vessel of the gods, must die after having served a sacred purpose. His death will teach his people the way of self-abasement before the divinity. His life is a sacrificial offering for the redemption of his fellow men. According to the prose essay and the last fragment, Empedokles is the chosen one 'in whom and through whom a world is resolved and renewed'. Thus everything leads up to this final consummation: the hero's death on Mount Etna. Its glory in the end far outshines its tragedy. We feel that the whole play has been written for the sake of the last great moments when Empedokles in the ecstasy of death exclaims:

O Iris' Bogen! über stürzenden
Gewässern, wenn die Wog' in Silberwolken
Auffliegt, wie du bist, so ist meine Freude!

This ending is for Hölderlin a solution to the problems with which he wrestled in *Hyperion*. By laying down his life Empedokles achieves the longed-for union with the divine without falling again into the sin of pride. Death alone restores the harmony between the two conflicting attributes of genius—heroism and humility. Death too enables genius to fulfil both his social mission and his mystical longing.

Yet, for all this, *Empedokles* is a baffling play. It poses a number of questions which cannot be answered satisfactorily. Can death be an act of penance for the hero's guilt and at the same time the fulfilment of his life? Is it conceivable that a Titan condemned for the sin of pride should be singled out for the role of saviour? Critics have tried to solve these difficulties by pointing out that Hölderlin changed his views in the course of writing his play. It is true that, in the last version, far greater emphasis is laid on the theme of redemption; but even there no attempt is made to disguise Empedokles' sin. The contradiction is, for Hölderlin, inherent in life itself. He sees sin as an inevitable part of the tragic

36

destiny of genius. Like Schiller, though in a different way, Hölderlin tries to reconcile the Greek idea of Fate with the Christian view of divine justice. Through genius, he believes, an apparent and momentary union with the deity is achieved, which, though it is sinful for the individual, is necessary for the progress of mankind. Genius, the agent of the dialectical process of history, has to transgress against the laws of moderation which govern the lives of ordinary men, in order to bring to a crisis the conflicts of his age and restore a healthy equilibrium. These views, in which the teaching of the historical Empedocles concerning the alternation of attraction and repulsion blend with Hegelian ideas, look forward to Hebbel's theory of tragedy. Yet Hölderlin's philosophy has neither the consistency nor the abstract rigidity of a system. For him history is a drama enacted by men and gods, and poetry its record.

The tragedy of *Empedokles* is modelled on the Greek religious drama. It is, however, fundamentally undramatic. Apart from the hero there are no interesting characters, and little action. Furthermore, the structure is weak and the motivation overcomplex. The significance of the play lies in the beauty and power of its language, which brings to mind that of the choruses of Greek tragedy. This is especially true of the last version. There is little of Hyperion's subjective romanticism in *Empedokles*. The death of Empedokles corresponds with the death of much of the ebullience of Hölderlin's immaturity. His vision, purged of personal emotion, is at once more immediate and more remote. As Empedokles awakens from sleep in the opening scene of the last version and enters upon his new course, these slow words resound with a grave and mysterious intensity:

> Euch ruf ich über das Gefild herein
> Vom langsamen Gewölk, ihr heissen Strahlen
> Des Mittags, ihr gereiftesten, dass ich
> An euch den neuen Lebenstag erkenne.
> Denn anders ist's wie sonst.

This is the diction of Hölderlin's mature poetry.

VII

The Mature Poetry: Themes and Problems

The period from the autumn of 1798 to the spring of 1800 which Hölderlin spent in Homburg was one of the most fruitful in his life. It was a time of intense concentration combined with stimulating social intercourse. Once again he was surrounded by a group of congenial friends. The centre of the Homburg circle was Isaak von Sinclair, of Scottish descent, a high official at the Court of the Landgrave of Homburg, who later represented his sovereign at the Congress of Vienna. Sinclair was a talented and versatile dilettante, who wrote plays, poetry and philosophical treatises, and who had been Hölderlin's most devoted friend since their student days in Jena. In Jena, too, Hölderlin had met Zwilling, son of the Homburg Court preacher; Zwilling was a soldier by profession, a great admirer of Napoleon (like Hölderlin himself) who gave his life in the service of his country in the Napoleonic wars; Zwilling was a philosopher by temperament, and his outlook had close affinities with Hölderlin's and Hegel's. Hegel himself belonged to the Homburg circle; so did Ebel (later to become the author of geological books), who was living mostly in Paris at that time, and provided his friends with political news from France. There was also the minor poet Siegfried Schmid (whom Schiller in a letter to Goethe mentions in the same breath with Hölderlin), Boehlendorff, the ill-fated playwright, and others. These names give some indication of the wide range of Hölderlin's interests; the intellectual atmosphere of Homburg was as animated as that of Tübingens some ten years previously.

Hölderlin himself was, during that period, mainly occupied with the study of Greek literature–his translations from Pindar probably date from this time–and with the technique of his craft. His chief concern was to discover a safe and 'sacred' formula, such as the ancients has possessed, which would fit the spirit of his own age and country. He arrived at some very original conclusions, which he wrote down in a number of essays and schemes for the different types of drama, epic, and lyric poetry. These essays, as well as the *Empedokles* fragments, Hölderlin intended for a new monthly journal which he planned to edit. It was be called *Iduna,* after the Germanic goddess of rejuvenation, and was to include articles on the *Iliad,* on the *Prometheus,* the *Antigone* and the *Œdipus,* on some of Horace's odes, the *Nouvelle Héloïse,* Shakespeare's *Antony and Cleopatra, Julius Caesar* and *Macbeth,* a new translation of *Ossian* (by a

38

friend of Hölderlin's), treatises on the subject of humanist education, etc. Hölderlin's publisher, however, was anxious to secure
the support of men of public renown before embarking upon this
venture. Hölderlin therefore appealed to some of his more celebrated friends, such as Schelling. Most of them never replied and
Schiller, from his own experience as editor, advised against the
plan. The project had to be abandoned; Hölderlin's last attempt
to establish himself as an independent writer had failed. The
years which followed, and which led up to his final illness, were
marked by an increasingly anxious and painful struggle to make
a living without having to enter the Church. Hölderlin's difficulties were aggravated by an inner conflict between his own
abhorrence for this course and his desire to spare his mother pain.

At last, when his funds were exhausted and his health im-
paired, Hölderlin returned home for a short visit and then pro-
ceeded to Stuttgart at the invitation of his friends Neuffer and
Landauer. The summer and the autumn of 1800 which he spent
there provided a brief interlude of happiness. He stayed at
Landauer's house, gave private tuition, and devoted the rest of his
time to his great hymns and elegies. However, the fear that the
ecclesiastical authorities might yet force him to accept a curacy
prompted him to take up another post as tutor in a private house.
In January 1801 he left for Hauptwyl near St Gallen, but returned to Nürtingen only a few months later, after being dismissed
by his employer. The rest of the year he spent partly at home and
partly in Stuttgart. In the autumn he accepted yet another post,
this time in Bordeaux. In December 1801 Hölderlin left home,
filled with a sense of foreboding, and bravely set out on foot on
the last journey of this kind he was ever to undertake. 'On the
dangerous snow-covered heights of Auvergne,' he wrote to his
mother after his arrival, 'in the storm and wilderness, during the
icy night, the charged pistol beside me on my rough couch, I
prayed a prayer which has been the best in my life up to now and
which I shall never forget.' (January 28th, 1802.) There was one
more letter to his mother from Bordeaux, in which he expressed
satisfaction with his new position. The next letter was from Nürtingen, dated December 2nd, 1802, and was addressed to Boehlendorff: 'I have not written to you for a long time. I have in the
meantime been to France, and have seen the sad, solitary earth,
the cottages of southern France, and men and women of great
personal beauty who have grown up in the fear of patriotic uncer-
tainty and of hunger. The mighty element, the fire from heaven,
and the calm of the people, their life in nature and their modest
condition and contentment have continually moved me, and as it

39

has been said of heroes, I may say that Apollo has struck me.' Early in July Hölderlin had suddenly appeared in Nürtingen showing signs of a severe mental disorder. Meanwhile, Susette Gontard had died in Frankfurt. It is not known when the news of her death reached him. It is possible that he passed through Frankfurt on his way back and learnt of it there. Altogether there is little reliable information about his return from France and the reasons for his departure. Hölderlin stayed with his mother from 1802 to 1804, entirely absorbed in his poetic work and in the study of Sophocles. He translated the *Œdipus Tyrannus* and the *Antigone* magnificently and arrestingly, forging what was almost a new language in his endeavour to recapture not only the spirit but also the diction and the rhythmical structure of the original. These two translations, prefaced by a profound study of Greek tragedy, were published in 1804. In July of that year Sinclair, who was not convinced that his friend was insane, brought him to Homburg. There he occupied the post of Court Librarian, an arrangement made in advance with the Landgrave by Sinclair, who paid the salary himself. For a short time Hölderlin seemed to recover, but he soon relapsed, and by 1806 his condition was such that Sinclair had to remove him. Much to Hölderlin's fury he was taken to a clinic, and in 1807 was set up in lodgings with a carpenter named Zimmer in Tübingen. There he remained for thirty-six years, occupying a small room in an old tower overlooking the banks of the Neckar. Many friends and sight-seers came to visit the poet, who, at that time, owed his popularity more to his mental derangement than to his works. Though unable to pursue any logical train of thought, Hölderlin preserved his poetic gifts to the last. The poems of those years are full of strangely simple and moving observations. Most of them are written in rhyme, which he had not used since his early period. In subject matter and form they show a complete break with his mature verse. Hölderlin died on June 7th, 1843.

Hölderlin's mature works comprise the poetry of the first Homburg period, the great poems of the years 1800 to 1801 (which include odes and hymns in archaic metres, several long elegies, and the first series of hymns in free verse) and finally the poems written after his return from Bordeaux, of which the best known are the hymns *Der Einzige* and *Patmos*, and the odes published in 1805 under the title of *Nachtgesänge*. These poems, in the words of his editor Hellingrath, represent 'the heart, core and peak of Hölderlin's works, the very legacy of the poet'. In spite of their diversity, they are linked by a common ideal and must be considered as a whole. Hölderlin was never concerned with the expression of a single, personal mood, but with the creation of an integral system. The universal quality of his work does not consist in the breadth and variety of his experience. Indeed Hölderlin's range is somewhat limited. His strength lies in the few basic themes which hold up the structure of his poetry like the pillars of a Gothic cathedral. All other elements are like crossbeams above which the pillars meet to form splendid arches. It is, however, only in its formal structure that Hölderlin's work can be compared to mediaeval architecture. The themes themselves are essentially rooted in the Renaissance.

The fusion of classical and Christian traditions which marks Hölderlin's poetry from the beginning is very pronounced in his mature works. For him the message of Love is the common legacy of both worlds. Throughout his poetry the word Love has both a platonic and a pietist connotation. He calls the Last Supper 'Abendmahl' the Banquet 'Gastmahl', for Last Supper and Banquet are both to him the 'Meal of Love' (Mahl der Liebe)–an expression used by Hegel in *Der Geist des Christentums*. The gods of Greece, like Christ himself, are Love incarnate; so too, in lesser degree, are the heroes, disciples and apostles.

Hölderlin's attitude to Christ was a complex one. In the late hymn *Der Einzige* he says that from early youth his love for Christ, his 'Master and Lord', has been stronger than his love for all the other gods. Indeed, his worship of the Greek gods themselves was always characterised by a Christian inwardness of feeling. It is therefore surprising that the figure of Christ should not appear until his later poetry. This can only be explained by his distaste for the Church and Christian dogma. The next world, original sin, good and evil, and even the cross, have no place in his spiritual universe. For Hölderlin life can be lived only in this world, transfigured though it is for him by the mystery of divine love. His vision of Christ's death and the meaning it has for him are contained in these words from *Patmos:*

> . . . nie genug
> Hatt' er, von Güte zu sagen,
> Der Worte, damals, und zu erheitern, da
> Er's sahe, das Zürnen der Welt.
> Denn alles ist gut. Drauf starb er. Vieles wäre
> Zu sagen davon. Und es sahn ihn, wie er siegend blickte,
> Den Freudigsten, die Freunde noch zuletzt.

His Christ has the radiant bearing of a Germanic hero combined with that look of touching and artless piety often found in mediaeval German art. This Christ-figure is sometimes merged in the Greek gods and heroes. Hölderlin tentatively introduced Christ in the guise of Empedokles, and, in the elegy *Brot und Wein,* as the wine-god Bacchus, while in the late hymn *Der Einzige* he openly declares him to be the brother of Bacchus and of Hercules. Christ, Bacchus and Hercules embody for Hölderlin the triumphant victory of love over suffering. The appearance of Christ for Hölderlin, as for Schelling (*Philosophie der Kunst*), is the climax of the classical era, and his death marks the end of the period.

The parallel between Christ and Hercules goes back to a mediaeval tradition. It is worked out in detail by Ronsard in his *Hercule Chrétien.* Michelangelo, in the *Last Judgment,* represents Christ as a Herculean figure, and Milton in *Paradise Regained* draws a parallel between the wrestling of Hercules and Anteus and the struggle of Christ and Satan (adding characteristically, however, 'to compare great things with small'). A comparison between the crucifixion and the burning of Hercules occurs in Hegel's *Vom Geist des Christentums.* The Christ-Bacchus analogy brings to mind Bellini's *Redeemer,* in the background of which are a number of pagan scenes including one depicting a bacchic sacrifice. But there was so little of orthodox Christianity in Hölderlin's composition that he placed Christ and the gods of Greece–almost–on the same level.

Like the poets of the Renaissance, Hölderlin sees the traditions of the past, Christian and pagan alike, in the light of a national revival. His humble invitation to the Greek Muses to come to Germany 'if the journey is not too long' (*Die Wanderung*) is a variation on a popular Renaissance theme. Over and over again it has reverberated through European literature since Petrarch addressed these proud words to Cola di Rienzo and the people of Rome: 'Crowned with the laurel of Apollo, I shall climb the heights of deserted Helicon and there, near the Castalian springs, recall the Muses from their exile'. Conrad Celtis's ode *Ad Apollinem repertorem poeticus: ut ab Italis cum lira ad Germanos veniat* marked the beginning of humanist poetry in Germany; but it was Klopstock who, more than any other writer of Hölderlin's time, stressed the importance of the Greeks and the Hebrew prophets in the re-awakening of the poetic genius of Germany.

For Hölderlin, as for Klopstock, Lessing and Herder, language was the instrument of national regeneration. In the hymn *Germania,* the eagle of God flies from the Indus across Parnassus, the Italian hills and the Swiss Alps to bring the chaste virgin, Germania, the divine gift of language. He finds her lying

... im Walde versteckt und blühendem Mohn
Voll süssen Schlummers,

but the god-sent gift, the 'Blume des Mundes' (flower of the mouth) as Hölderlin calls it, awakens her and she begins to speak. Addressing her proudly the poet goes on to say:

... Fülle der goldenen Worte sandtest du auch,
Glückselige, mit den Strömen, und sie quillen unerschöpflich
In die Gegenden all.

These words, too, which are spoken in Hölderlin's inimitable idiom, echo the Renaissance cult of the vernacular.

For Hölderlin the link between past and present is genius. In his eyes the genius is a god-like creature, and the historical panorama of his poetry consists in a chain of these beings rising like single luminous peaks in a mountain range which stretches from prehistoric times down to the poet's own age. In the distance are the gods of Olympus, whose origins point far back into the mysterious Asiatic past, and nearer at hand Christ, last offspring of the ancient gods. These stand nearest to the 'Highest' or the 'Father' or 'the God' as Hölderlin sometimes calls him. Next come the men of genius: biblical prophets, patriarchs, disciples and apostles, as well as Greek Titans, heroes and philosophers. They are followed by the great figures of the poet's own age, outstanding among which are Rousseau and Napoleon. According to late plans and sketches, the gap between antiquity and modern times was to be filled by poems about Mohammed, the German Emperors Henry IV, Barbarossa, Konradin of Swabia, Columbus and Luther. Finally there are the various *genii loci*, the genii of nature and of love, and, of course, the poet. He who is filled with the spirit of genius brings the message of genius to mankind. It is genius, and more particularly poetic genius, which hears and interprets the divine voice proclaiming its message through the clashes and storms of history. Endowed with the gift of divination:

Kennt er im ersten Zeichen Vollendetes schon,
Und fliegt, der kühne Geist, wie Adler den
Gewittern, weissagend seinen
Kommenden Göttern voraus.

(Rousseau)

43

Thunder and lightning, with their rich biblical and mythological associations, are Hölderlin's favourite symbols of revelation. They are therefore connected with the appearance of a god or a genius: with Christ, Empedokles, Bacchus and the poet. Hölderlin's vision of the poetic mission culminates in the stanza of *Wie wenn am Feiertage*, where the poet stands fearlessly exposed to the heavenly lightning, and with his bare hands grasps the burning missile of the gods.

> Doch uns gebührt es, unter Gottes Gewittern,
> Ihr Dichter! mit entblösstem Haupte zu stehen,
> Des Vaters Strahl, ihn selbst, mit eigner Hand
> Zu fassen und dem Volk, ins Lied
> Gehüllt, die himmlische Gabe zu reichen.

The terror of revelation is followed by the holy gladness of the 'Feier' (feast) which restores peace and repose. The 'Feier' is at the same time a mystical 'Brautfest' (bridal feast) of men and gods and a sociable festival of the people, with songs and wreaths and community celebrations. The festive spirit is for Hölderlin the basis of all civilisation.

The landscape of Hölderlin's mature poetry is topographical and symbolical at the same time. Everything has its being concurrently in space, time and eternity. His grandiose geographical symbolism embraces all those countries of Indo Germanic civilisation which meant so much to him: India, the glowing and luxuriant coast of Asia Minor, the Greek Archipelago and Athens, all bathed in a silvery light, the Swiss Alps, 'the castle of the gods', southern France and South Germany with its great rivers, the Danube, the Rhine, the Main and the Neckar, with its hills and dales, its woods and fertile fields. This landscape, itself saturated with the spirit of genius, forms the background against which Hölderlin's heroes and gods stand out in all their grandeur. It is inhabited by the graceful spirits of Greece and Swabia, as well as the subterranean powers which drive the rivers in their impetuous flow towards the ocean and break out from the volcanic depths of the earth. They all recall the divine origin of life, and lead all created things back towards their source. Nature in these poems is neither quite the Creation as in the early works nor the loving reflection of the human heart as in *Hyperion*: it is rather a system of divine hieroglyphs which the poet has to decipher. In this attitude to nature, too, Hölderlin shows himself a true son of the Renaissance. He belonged to the last generation for whom this Renaissance conception of nature prevailed. It underlies the fascination which maps always had for Hölderlin–his walls were covered with them–and the geographical symbolism of his work. It informs the geological observations of Ebel, the nature philosophy of Schelling, and the scientific investigations of Goethe and Novalis.

Hölderlin's endeavour, then, was to arrive at a great Renaissance synthesis of history, nature, and religious tradition. He stands with Goethe as the foremost poetic genius of the Renaissance in Germany. Like Goethe, though in a different way, he marks the late flowering of the Renaissance during the age of European romanticism. The works of both poets are permeated with the deeply unsettling, romantic spirit of their period. In Hölderlin's work we find, strangely intermingled with the most fervid faith, expressions of heartsearching anxiety. Every theme of his mature poetry is fraught with conflict.

His hopes of an imminent religious revival alternated with feelings of despair. From the time of *Hyperion,* in spite of his visionary faith, he saw his age in a gloomy light. In a fragment entitled *Neue Welt,* he gives this description of modern times:

> und es hängt, ein ehern Gewölbe, der Himmel über uns, es lähmt Fluch die Glieder der Menschen, und die erfreuenden Gaben der Erde sind wie Spreu, es spottet unser mit ihren Geschenken die Mutter und alles ist Schein.

In *Der Archipelagus* the age appears as an enormous, joyless factory:

> ... weh! es wandelt in Nacht, es wohnt, wie im Orkus,
> Ohne Göttliches unser Geschlecht. An's eigene Treiben
> Sind sie geschmiedet allein, und sich in der tosenden Werkstatt
> Höret Jeglicher nur, und viel arbeiten die Wilden
> Mit gewaltigem Arm, rastlos, doch immer und immer
> Unfruchtbar, wie die Furien, bliebt die Mühe der Armen.

There is no sanctuary, no centre of worship:

> Herzen schlagen und doch bleibet die Rede zurück.

The gods themselves have vanished. Among the last fragments there are frightening visions of the age as a labyrinthic wilderness in which man gropes blindly and vainly for a way out.

The recurrent symbol of the age which at times he has hailed as the dawn of a new era is night. The entire period following the decline of the Greek world and the appearance of Christ is por-

45

trayed in Hölderlin's mature poetry as a period of night. Over
and over again he asks: what is night? Night must have a meaning
and a purpose; indeed, it must be sacred, for it has been ordained
by the gods. Here, too, humble resignation and intense distress
alternate.

In the odes of the early Homburg period these fluctuations of
mood are comparatively simple. In *Abendphantasie* the vision
of the setting sun calls forth this sequence:

> Am Abendhimmel blühet ein Frühling auf;
> Unzählig blühn die Rosen, und ruhig scheint
> Die goldne Welt; o dorthin nehmt mich,
> Purpurne Wolken . . .

> Doch, wie verscheucht von törichter Bitte, flieht
> Der Zauber; dunkel wirds, und einsam
> Unter dem Himmel, wie immer, bin ich–

> Komm du nun, sanfter Schlummer . . .

With this modest acceptance of unfulfilled longing and with the
prospect of peace and old age the ode closes.

In the later poems, the spiritual conflicts are more violent,
more complex and more persistent. In the elegy *Brot und Wein*,
for example, the dreamlike vision of the radiant past conjured up
during the dark hours of night is constantly interrupted by lamentations over the present.

> Aber Freund, wir kommen zu spät. Zwar leben die Götter,
> Aber über dem Haupt droben in anderer Welt.
> Endlos wirken sie da und scheinen's wenig zu achten,
> Ob wir leben,

and Hölderlin continues with the surprising turn,

> so sehr schonen die Himmlischen uns.
> Denn nicht immer vermag ein schwaches Gefäss sie zu fassen,
> Nur zu Zeiten erträgt göttliche Fülle der Mensch.

In the middle of the sentence Hölderlin has veered round from
what is almost an accusation to an expression of thankfulness.

The crucial question in Hölderlin's poetry, however, is the
plight of the modern poet held back from the fulfilment of his
devinely appointed mission. Schiller's lament 'And for us there

46

remained the soulless word' is echoed more despairingly by
Hölderlin:

> So zu harren und was zu tun indess und zu sagen,
> Weiss ich nicht und wozu Dichter in dürftiger Zeit?

Does not an age like his own, Hölderlin asks, destroy the very
basis of poetry? Yet does it not at the same time need the poet
more desperately than ever? These conflicting stresses are at the
root of all Hölderlin's works. In *Brot und Wein* he finds consolation in pinning his faith to night itself. He strives to resign himself to night with all its manifold and contradictory implications.
Night is the dark passage between the light of yesterday and the
light of to-morrow, a power which is sacred in its own right, the
period of forgetfulness and commemoration, of peace and intoxication, of slumber and vigilance. Finally, night is a time
hallowed by the gods themselves; for did not the wine-god
Bacchus, bringer of joy, and Christ, god of reconciliation, de-
scend even into the darkest night of Hades? The answer to the
question: 'Wozu Dichter in dürftiger Zeit?' which persists
throughout the poem, is given in the lines which immediately
follow:

> Aber sie sind, sagst du, wie des Weingotts heilige Priester,
> Welche von Lande zu Land zogen in heiliger Nacht.

In *Der blinde Sänger* the theme of night is linked with that
of the poet's blindness. The ode opens with the invocation to
light, followed by the words from the *Song of Songs* 'my heart is
awake', which ring sorrowfully through the darkness. The poet
recalls the happy times of youth before he was struck blind, when
he could see the 'blissful pinions of heaven' sailing over the earth.
Now he is alone and only through the memory of the past can he
conjure up visions. They are the creations of his 'thought', not
the gifts of inspiration, and he indulges in them 'for his own joy',
not for the sake of mankind. Anxiously he listens for the distant
voice of the thunder, the voice of the god. It draws nearer and
nearer until, at last, it breaks through the silence and:

> Ihm nach, ihr meine Saiten! es lebt mit ihm
> Mein Lied, und wie die Quelle dem Strome folgt,
> Wohin er denkt, so muss ich fort und
> Folge dem Sicheren auf der Irrbahn.

47

The poet's eyesight is restored, day breaks over 'down-tumbling clouds', a radiance pours down, more spiritual than the light of childhood, and the world is transfigured.

The late ode *Chiron*, one of the *Nachtgesänge*, is a new version of *Der blinde Sänger*. Here the symbol of the blinded seer is replaced by that of the hybrid centaur. The wise centaur Chiron, skilled, according to tradition, in the healing arts of medicine, has been maimed not by blindness but by the poisoned arrow of the gods. He, too, is a symbol of the poet. His wound is a divine visitation, so that his very torment is an ecstasy. In apocalyptic visions Chiron beholds the universe, while the god of thunder descends earthwards to purge the world. Yet, as the storm passes, a new transparent and strangely sharp light breaks from the skies, and everything has its right place and order. Chiron is healed, he is now sure of his gift of prophecy.

This poem, in spite of the mysterious clarity of its end, conveys the experience of an almost unbearable strain and torment. The same note is found in much of Hölderlin's later work. The sublime vision of his calling and the impossibility of fulfilling it in his own age weigh him down with anxiety. The poet's mission is, indeed, a perilous one. Like Pindar, Hölderlin believes that innocence is his only shield, but there is always the risk that he may overreach himself and bring down upon his own head the avenging wrath of the gods. The fear of what has been previously described as pseudo-mysticism is ever present in the later poems. It is always felt in those moments when genius

> Verwegenes erwählt
> Und den Göttern gleich zu werden getrachet.

The poet cannot always be sure of inspiration. If he speaks without divine authority, it is as though he were presuming to give an answer where no question had been asked (*Der Mutter Erde*).

Then, too, the poet may err in the opposite direction. He may be over-timid. It is his duty boldly to obey the heavenly call. He must not lack courage. In *Dichtermut* and its later version *Blödigkeit*, in *Ermunterung* and in *Dichterberuf*, Hölderlin tries to reassure himself. The very titles of these odes are revealing. They affirm once again the glory of his vocation. Thus the poet's great difficulty is to strike the balance between heroism and humility.

The most powerful contrapuntal development of the two themes is the hymn *Der Rhein*. Here the heroic impulse is that of the river Rhine, which again and again is curbed by the gods. The following stanza with its great rhythmic swell and its magic

vision is perhaps Hölderlin's finest evocation of genius gushing
forth from its source:

> Drum ist ein Jauchzen sein Wort.
> Nicht liebt er, wie andere Kinder,
> In Wickelbanden zu weinen;
> Denn, wo die Ufer zuerst
> An die Seit' ihm schleichen, die krummen,
> Und durstig umwindend ihn,
> Den Unbedachten, zu ziehn
> Und wohl zu behüten begehren
> Im eigenen Zahne, lachend
> Zerreisst er die Schlangen und stürzt
> Mit der Beut', und wenn in der Eil'
> Ein Grösserer ihn nicht zähmt,
> Ihn wachsen lässt, wie der Blitz, muss er
> Die Erde spalten, und wie Bezauberte fliehn
> Die Wälder ihm nach und zusammensinkend die Berge.

Smiling at this youthful violence, the gods set to work to tame
the spirit of genius. They throw obstacles in his way and mould
him in a tunnel of iron. In this way the torrential river becomes
the friendly 'Father Rhine' and follows the course laid down for
him in tranquility of spirit:

> ... wenn er das Land baut,
> Der Vater Rhein, und liebe Kinder nährt
> In Städten, die er gegründet.

It would not be Hölderlin's way to end the poem here. The river
swells and boils, is checked and swells again, until, in the end,
night falls. Gods and men celebrate their 'bridal feast'. At last
this, too, comes to an end and the river flows into the ocean,
when, in Hölderlin's own words:

> ... alles gemischt
> Ist, ordnungslos, und wiederkehrt
> Uralte Verwirrung.

The reconciliation achieved here is not steadily maintained. Hölderlin looked to tradition for guidance and support. *Patmos*
shows the poet's journey to that Greek island of the Revelation
of St John in search of living traces of Christ's presence. The
subject of this hymn is the death of Christ, the terror of divine

absence experienced by the disciples and the poet himself, combined with a sense of God's everlasting presence. Interwoven
with this theme is that of the poet's mission. The intensity of his
longing for Christ's return makes him for a moment feel that he
has the power,

> Ein Bild zu bilden und ähnlich
> Zu schaun, wie er gewesen, den Christ.

Yet this pride has provoked the wrath of God, who has appeared
to the poet in a vision and told him to be humble. The closing
lines of the hymn proclaim that the true mission of the poet is to
interpret the past:

> der Vater aber liebt,
> Der über allen waltet,
> Am meisten, dass gepfleget werde
> Der feste Buchstab' und Bestehendes gut
> Gedeutet. Dem folgt deutscher Gesang.

There is a ring of finality in these words; for this reason they have
been regarded as expressing Hölderlin's ultimate belief, the
renunciation of prophetic poetry and the humble obedience to
tradition. Yet against these lines of *Patmos* stand the even later
fragments *Aus dem Motivkreis der Titanen*, with their praise of
the Titans as the helpmates of the gods, and the ode on Gany-
mede, the divine cupbearer. Hölderlin does not resolve the ten-
sion; it remains to the last the very pulse of his poetry.

The poems of the latest period reveal yet another disturbing
conflict, which is latent in Hölderlin's work from the beginning,
but which has not previously been directly faced. His allegiance
to both the gods of Greece and to Christ now appears to him in a
problematic light. The anxious desire to give just praise to all the
gods and the fear that he may, after all, not be able to reconcile
their conflicting claims are the theme of *Der Einzige*. In this hymn,
in which Hölderlin proclaims Christ as the brother of Hercules
and Bacchus, he confesses:

> Es hindert aber eine Scham
> Mich, dir zu vergleichen
> Die weltlichen Männer.

It is the most naïve as well as the most painful expression of the
difficulty in which the dual European heritage involves the poet,

50

The end of the poem is an attempt to unite all the conflicting opposites. Christ is seen as God imprisoned in the world. Thus the poet belonging to both worlds and linking the two traditions might be said to follow in Christ's footsteps. This is what the last words of *Der Einzige* may be interpreted to mean:

> Die Dichter müssen auch
> Die geistigen, weltlich sein.

Hölderlin's poetry conveys a dual experience: the presence of the divine and man's difficulty in apprehending it. The introductory lines of *Patmos* express in one monumental sentence both aspects of this experience, linking them by the simple word 'and'. The landscape of the first stanza of this hymn, with its closely gathered peaks, its abysses and bridges, is the best description of Hölderlin's spiritual universe.

> Nah ist
> Und schwer zu fassen der Gott.
> Wo aber Gefahr ist, wächst
> Das Rettende auch.
> In Finstern wohnen
> Die Adler und furchtlos gehn
> Die Söhne der Alpen über den Abgrund weg
> Auf leichtgebaueten Brücken.
> Drum, da gehäuft sind rings
> Die Gipfel der Zeit,
> Und die Liebsten nahe wohnen, ermattend auf
> Getrenntesten Bergen,
> So gib unschuldig Wasser,
> O Fittiche gib uns, treuesten Sinns
> Hinüberzugehn und wiederzukehren.

VIII

The Mature Poetry: Language and Form

Although Hölderlin's poetry is in some sense the poetry of ideas, he was not a man of powerful intellect. There is no clearly defined hierarchy of values in his verse, nor does he achieve a real intellectual mastery of the problems with which he is obsessed. But his poems reveal a powerful awareness of spiritual reality. For all the doubts and despair expressed in them, they are imbued with a sense of divine presence. Indeed, Hölderlin's mature works have something of the fire, the stark and uncompromising immediacy of religious experience which are to be found in the Bible and in Greek literature. This is not merely due to the fact that the biblical writers, Pindar, Sophocles, Horace, and Klopstock, were his masters. His early poems have been inspired by these same models, without recapturing their spirit. It was only when, after subordinating these influences to his personal emotions, he attained a level of consciousness deeper than emotion, that he was able to reanimate the symbols of antiquity. Only then could he conjure them up from the depths of his own experience. This affinity with antiquity sprang from Hölderlin's essential primitiveness. His thought was often involved, but his intuition was elemental. For him the division between inner and outer reality, so characteristic of modern man, did not exist. His poetry is concerned neither with the nature of the world nor with the moods and passions of man. His subject, like that of the poets of antiquity, is the encounter between human and divine forces. It is as though Hölderlin, like them, has met the gods face to face. The concreteness of his poetry, like theirs, is the concreteness of spiritual fact.

Peace approaches him in the visible form of a god. This divine apparition makes his knees tremble, and he has to grope his way towards it like a man blinded by a sudden radiance. Like Job, like the heroes of Greece, the poet is wounded by the arrows of God. The divine spirit literally seizes him by the hair. The air resounds with calls going to and fro between men and gods; the world is filled with messengers and voices.

The first movement of the elegy *Heimkunft* illustrates Hölderlin's vision of this incessant communication between heaven and earth. Nature appears here as a gigantic workshop:

Drin in den Alpen ist's noch helle Nacht, und die Wolke,
Freudiges dichtend, sie deckt drinnen das gähnende Tal.
Dahin, dorthin, toset und stürzt die scherzende Bergluft,
Schroff durch die Tannen herab glänzet und schwindet ein Strahl;
Langsam eilt und kämpft das freudigschauernde Chaos,
Jung an Gestalt, doch stark, feiert es liebenden Streit
Unter den Felsen, es gährt und wankt in den ewigen Schranken,
Denn bacchantischer zieht drinnen der Morgen herauf.
Denn es wächst unendlicher dort das Jahr, und die heilgen
Stunden, die Tage, sie sind kühner geordnet, gemischt.
Dennoch merket die Zeit der Gewittervogel, und zwischen
Bergen, hoch in der Luft weilt er und rufet den Tag.

52

Jetzt auch wachet und schaut in der Tiefe drinnen das Dörflein,
Furchtlos, Hohem vertraut, unter den Gipfeln hinauf,
Wachstum ahnend, denn schon, wie Blitze, fallen die alten
Wasserquellen, der Grund unter den Stürzenden dampft,
Echo tönet umher, und die unermessliche Werkstatt
Reget bei Tag und Nacht, Gaben versendend, den Arm!

If we look into Hölderlin's own workshop and try to analyse
the elements of his vision, we find that it can best be described in
terms of a blending of opposites. This is true quite apart from his
obvious preference for oxymorons. Hölderlin seizes upon single
phenomena such as the precipitous fall of the cataract, and ren-
ders them with extraordinary sharpness. His late poetry in particular is a network of sharply etched lines. Yet the total impression of his landscape is anything but linear. It is rather one of
surging masses of light and form. The mountains, the clouds, the
birds are universal rather than specific; so are the processes of
nature: the change from night to day, the passing of the hours,
the growth of organic matter.

Another characteristic blending of opposites is to be found in
Hölderlin's attitude to the divinity, which is in part a childlike
and joyous intimacy and in part an awed sense of the *tremendum*.
Whilst the clouds and winds are jesting and the little village looks
up freely to the familiar heights, there are gaping abysses nearby
and formidable powers are being unleashed. There is a primitive
apprehension of the co-existence of benevolence and menace in
nature. Innocence and terror live side by side, and together
constitute Hölderlin's particular experience of holiness.

The evocation of holiness is his chief concern. Perhaps no
other poet conveys the ineffable purity of holiness so delicately
and with such naïve reverence:

Ruhig glänzen indess die silbernen Höhen darüber,
Voll mit Rosen ist schon droben der leuchtende Schnee,
Und noch höher hinauf wohnt über dem Lichte der reine,
Selige Gott vom Spiel heiliger Strahlen erfreut.

These lines which open the second movement of *Heimkunft*
follow upon the bacchantic vision of the rising day in the first
movement. Whenever the divinity is apprehended as a dynamic
force Hölderlin's language takes on daemonic violence. The note
of intoxication apparent from his earliest period is most glorious-
ly sounded in *Der blinde Sänger*, in the frantic headlong rush of
the spellbound river in *Der Rhein*, in *Der Archipelagus*, where

. . . am heissen Gestad die gewittertrunkenen Wälder
Rauschen und wogen,

or in this description of a festive procession in *Stuttgart:*

Und wie Wagen, bespannt mit freiem Wilde, so ziehen die
Berge voran, und so träget und eilet der Pfad.

The ethereal and the dionysian manifestations of the gods and his
own sense of innocence and of terror are for Hölderlin complementary.

The mystery of divine presence so strongly conveyed by his
language is the mystery of reality itself. Its impact is immediate
and novel. With Hölderlin we often feel that a spiritual reality
has taken him by surprise, and his poetry is always filled with his
own sense of wonder, as divinity approaches him from an unknown realm and mysteriously unfolds before his eyes. The most
sublime expression of this experience is to be found in the last
stanzas of *Der Abschied* (third version) and in this passage from
Brot und Wein, where a faint draught of air, a pure spiritual
messenger, heralds in a magic night with its cortège of light,
silence and sadness:

Jetzt auch kommet ein Wehn und regt die Gipfel des Hains auf,
Sieh! und das Schattenbild unserer Erde, der Mond
Kommet geheim nun auch; die Schwärmerische, die Nacht
                                                    kommt,
Voll mit Sternen und wohl wenig bekümmert um uns,
Glänzt die Erstaunende dort, die Fremdlingin unter den
                                                    Menschen
Über Gebirgeshöhn traurig und prächtig herauf.

In the later hymns the colour background is no longer a transparent silver but rich glowing gold and purple. We find a bewilder-
ing concreteness, which is not less mysteriously spiritual for all
its profuse sensual awareness. The vision of Asia in *Patmos* is
characteristic of the splendour of this later style:

Doch bald, in frischem Glanze,
Geheimnisvoll
Im goldenen Rauche blühte,
Schnell aufgewachsen
Mit Schritten der Sonne,
Mit tausend Gipfeln duftend

54

Mir Asia auf, und geblendet sucht'
Ich eines, das ich kennete, denn ungewohnt
War ich der breiten Gassen, wo herab
Vom Tmolus fährt
Der goldgeschmückte Pactol
Und Taurus stehet und Messogis,
Und voll von Blumen der Garten,
Ein stilles Feuer. Aber im Lichte
Blüht hoch der silberne Schnee;
Und Zeug' unsterblichen Lebens
An unzugangbaren Wänden
Uralt der Epheu wächst und getragen sind
Von lebenden Säulen, Zedern und Lorbeern,
Die feierlichen, die göttlichgebauten Paläste.

The power of this poetry is, of course, due as much to the music
of its language and the beauty of its structure as to the vision it
imparts. In the passages quoted there is an exquisite balance
between the arresting effect of the inversions and appositions on
the one hand and the long cumulative periods and *enjambement*
of lines and stanzas on the other. This tidal flow becomes increasingly marked in the later poems. Words and parts of speech
often lie like breakwaters across the current of the sentences.
More and more the single word stands out in significant relief.

Another means of arresting the movement of the sentence is
the frequent use of subordinate clauses. They abound in the late
hymns where the language, as ragged as the mountainous landscape at the beginning of *Patmos*, has to force its way through a
maze of intervening conjunctions. The opposite tendency, however, the increasing lengthening of periods and stanzas, is equally
apparent.

The metre, too, has the dual effect of precipitating and hinder-
ing the flow. Hölderlin is very strict in his use of the traditional
asclepiads, alcaics, and hexameters. His thorough metrical
training can be felt even in the free rhythms of the later hymns.
These are divided into stanzas of fixed lengths, and an attempt
has been made to discover precise laws governing the arrangement of stanzas within each hymn and for groups of hymns
respectively. There is no doubt that all but the very late poems
show a conscious control of form which counterbalances the
dithyrambic vehemence of the language.

The structure of the whole poem, however, derives from what
Hölderlin calls 'der Rhythmus der Vorstellungen' (the rhythm of
ideas). It is determined by the rhythmic sequence inherent in his

55

ideas and experiences themselves. Hölderlin's poems are not, like most of those of the romantics, focussed on one set of experiences. Not only are they much more complex, but they also lack the focal point; they have no foreground or background, in short no perspective. Nor have they a decorative pattern like the odes and hymns of Pindar, for they lack the very basis of that kind of poetry—an abundant and varied mythology. Hölderlin confines himself to a few mythological and historical figures and a number of fixed symbols. It is round these figures and symbols that he groups his experiences, charging each of them with complex significance and swiftly moving from one set of symbols to another. Every symbol is like a star emitting rays in all directions, which link up with the radiations of other symbols, so that there emerges a network of symbolic significances. By this rich interweaving of a few central symbols Hölderlin finds a modern substitute for mythology. His contrapuntal arrangement of symbolical groups is determined by the rhythm of his experiences. It is the inner rhythm of his poetry which establishes the balance between those conflicts of heroism and humility, faith and doubt, which so tormented Hölderlin. He has mastered them—not so much on the level of conscious thought as in terms of the rhythms they engender.

To Hölderlin the rhythm of language meant the revelation of the spirit through the medium of poetry. In her book *Die Günderode,* Bettina Brentano records some remarks which the poet made at a time when he was already mentally deranged, and which were communicated to her by Sinclair: 'He who is educated for poetry in the divine sense has to acknowledge the spirit of the Highest as a lawless force set above himself and must abandon the law for it. Not as I will but as Thou wilt . . . If poetry is bound by the law the spirit can only rock itself on a swing, grasping two ropes, and merely seeming to fly . . . But the eagle who does not measure his flight . . . his soul, being compelled by secret forces to escape self-consciousness in the very moment of his highest consciousness, thereby safeguards the life of the spirit—in him the spirit hatches itself out and learns to soar, often carried away by the sacred rhythm, then borne along, swung up and down in sacred frenzy, abandoned to the divine; for this only comes from within: the movement towards the sun; it clings to the rhythm'.

It was not until the twentieth century that Hölderlin's mature poetry was re-discovered; but once Stefan George and his circle had opened the ears of their contemporaries to the uniqueness of his language, Hölderlin was quickly recognised as one of the great masters of the age. For Stefan George, the chief bond between the older poet and himself was the poetic ideal and the use of words. Poets like Trakl and Albrecht Schäffer were deeply influenced by Hölderlin's rhythms as well as by his diction. Only the late work of Rilke, however, shows a complete assimilation of Hölderlin's use of poetic devices: rhythm, diction, complexity and arrangement of symbols, contrapuntal structure—they all reveal a kindred tendency. In England, too, where Hölderlin has become known thanks to a number of translations and critical works, the recognition of his genius coincides with a conception of poetic language and form which is closely related to his own.

APPENDIX

1770, March 20th:	Hölderlin born in Lauffen, Württemberg.
1774-84	Attends Grammar School at Nürtingen.
1784-86	Attends Lower Monastery School at Denkendorf.
1786-88	Attends Higher Monastery School at Maulbronn.
1788-93	Attends Theological Seminary at Tübingen. Forms friendship with Neuffer and Magenau; they found Poetry Club. From 1790 Hölderlin on terms of friendship with Hegel and Schelling. Attains status of 'Magister'. Passes final examination before the Royal Consistory at Stuttgart. *Works:* Tübingen hymns. *Die Geschichte der schönen Künste unter den Griechen. Die Parallele zwischen Salomons Sprichwörtern und Hesiods Werken und Tagen.*
1793	Appointed tutor to son of Charlotte von Kalb in Waltershausen near Jena. *Works:* Preliminary work on *Hyperion.*
1794, Autumn:	Arrives in Jena. Attends Fichte's lectures. Maintains friendship with Schiller. *Works:* Several hymns Early fragment of *Hyperion.*
1795, Summer:	Returns to Nürtingen. Renews contact with Schelling.
December:	Appointed tutor to Gontard children in Frankfurt. Falls in love with Susette Gontard.
1797	Hegel takes post as tutor in Frankfurt. Hölderlin interviewed by Goethe at Schiller's request. *Works:* First part of *Hyperion* published. Work on *Empedokles* in progress until 1800.
1798, Autumn:	Leaves Frankfurt for Homburg. Corresponds with Susette Gontard and meets her secretly. Forms friendship with Isaak von Sinclair and others. Embarks on intensive study of Greek literature. *Works:* Homburg odes in progress until 1800. Philosophical essays in progress until 1800.
1799:	Plans for the journal *Iduna.* *Works:* Second part of *Hyperion* published.

58

1800, Spring	Returns to Nürtingen.
Summer	Stays with Landauer in Stuttgart.
and	*Works:* Odes and hymns in archaic meters, most
Autumn:	of the elegies, and first cycle of hymns in free verse in progress until 1801.
1801, January:	Appointed tutor to Gonzenbach children in Hauptwyl near St Gallen.
April:	Returns to Nürtingen.
Rest of year:	Spends part of his time at home and part at Stuttgart.
1802, January:	Appointed tutor to the family of a Hamburg consul at Bordeaux.
May:	Leaves Bordeaux.
June 22nd:	Susette Gontard dies in Frankfurt.
July:	Arrives in Nürtingen in state of mental disorder. *Works:* Hymns *Der Einzige* and *Patmos.* Translations from Sophocles in progress.
1804:	Taken by Sinclair to Homburg, where he becomes Court Librarian. *Works:* Translations of the *Œdipus Tyrannus* and of the *Antigone* published.
1805:	Mental condition deteriorates. *Works: Nachtgesänge* published.
1806:	Taken to clinic at Tübingen.
1807:	Lodges with carpenter Zimmer in Tübingen.
1843, June 7th:	Hölderlin dies.

SELECT BIBLIOGRAPHY

EDITIONS

Hölderlin, sämtliche Werke, historisch-kritische Ausgabe. Begonnen durch Norbert v. Hellingrath, fortgeführt durch Friedrich Seebass und Ludwig v. Pigenot:
  2nd edition, 6 vols, *Berlin*, 1923
  3rd edition, vols 1-4, *Berlin*, 1943
(Quotations in this essay have been taken from this edition. The spelling has been modernised.)
Friedrich Hölderlin, sämtliche Werke und Briefe. Kritisch-historische Ausgabe von Franz Zinkernagel, 5 vols, *Leipzig*, 1914-26.
Atlantis-Ausgabe von Hölderlins Werken, 2 vols, *Zürich*, 1944.
Friedrich Hölderlin, Gedichte, selected and edited by A. Closs, *London*, 1942.

TRANSLATIONS

Poems of Hölderlin, translated by Michael Hamburger, *London*, 1943·
Friedrich Hölderlin, Selected Poems, translated by J. B. Leishman, *London*, 1944.
Some Poems of Friedrich Hölderlin, translated by Frederic Prokosch, *Norfolk, Connecticut, U.S.A.*, 1943.
The Archipelago, translated by J. B. Leishman, *London*, 1947.

SOME CRITICAL STUDIES

BERTAUX, P.: Le lyrisme mythique de Hölderlin, *Paris*, 1936
BÖCKMAN, P.: Hölderlin und seine Götter, *München*, 1935.
GUARDINI, R.: Hölderlin, Weltbild und Frömmigkeit, *Leipzig*, 1939.
KEMPTER, L.: Hölderlin und die Mythologie, *Zürich*, 1929.
MÜLLER, E.: Hölderlin, Studien zur Geschichte seines Geistes, *Stuttgart*, 1944.
PEACOCK, R.: Hölderlin, *London*, 1938.
STAHL, E. L.: Hölderlin's Symbolism, *Oxford*, 1945.
STAIGER, E.: Der Geist der Liebe und das Schicksal. Schelling, Hegel und Hölderlin, *Leipzig*, 1935.
STANSFIELD, A.: Hölderlin, *Manchester*, 1944.

ENGLISH TRANSLATIONS OF PASSAGES
QUOTED IN THE TEXT

p. 8. Is this then the holy way? Oh! glorious vision, do not deceive me. Is it this path I tread, borne aloft on the high-flying morning cloud of song?

p. 12. I carry God's image within me. If He desires to see Himself then He can do so only in me or in those like me. God is the fire within me and I am His reflection, are we not then intimately at one?

p. 12. Friendless was the great Lord of the universe. He felt that something was lacking, therefore He created minds, blissfully mirroring His blessedness.

p. 16. The bowl of life has brimmed over, brooks and suns follow their course; young valleys, drunk with love, cling to the loving hills.

p. 16. What art thou, earth? chides the ocean, what art thou? do I not stretch out my arms over the weak one as the eagle stretches his pinions over the deer?

p. 18. As the eagle on the grey cliff is seized by a wild longing for the stars.

p. 19. As when the poet sat under Tibur's trees and in divine dreams forgot the passage of the years, when he was shaded by the elm tree and when the waters of Anio played, proud and gay, among silver blossoms, and as in Plato's halls when, welcomed by nightingales, the star of love shone through the greenwood, when the air was heavy with sleep and, gently stirred by a swan, Cephissus flowed by olive tree and myrtle bush: the earth is still as beautiful. Our hearts, too, knew the life and peace of friendly nature. The glorious sky still blossoms, the sounds of spring still blend with the song of our heart.

Seek then in the quietest valley the most fragrant grove, and pour from a golden bowl the glad sacrificial wine. The fresh image of the earth still smiles upon you, you and I are still watched over by the God of Youth.

p. 22. Where is Germany? I cannot find that land: where the intellectual sphere begins, the political ends.

p. 23. And for us there remained the soulless word.

p. 24. She is dead who brought me up and nursed me, dead is now the youthful world.

p. 24. The joyous certainty of finding the loyal bond stronger still and more mature; that bond which was not sealed by any oath: to live only for freedom and truth and never, never to come to terms with such dogma as may restrain opinion and sentiment.

p. 25. But we, happily side by side, like the loving swans who rest on the lake or, rocked by the waves, gaze down into the waters, where silvery clouds are reflected and ethereal blue swells beneath them as they glide—thus we walked on earth. And though the North Wind—the enemy of lovers, the bearer of grief—might threaten, and though the leaves fell from the branches and the rain was driven by the wind, we smiled serenely, feeling the presence of our god in the intimacy of communion in the one song of our hearts, perfectly at peace, alone with ourselves, childlike and happy.

p. 29. It is as though I saw, but then fear seizes me as though it were my own form that I had seen. It is as though I had felt the spirit of the universe, but then I awoke, and it seems as though I had been holding my own fingers.

p. 29. Only you who are eternally young can nourish a childlike faith in the hearts of those who love you, and can save misguided and despairing genius from pining away its life.

p. 33. I bring together disparate things, my word gives a name to that which was unknown, and I carry the love of living beings back and forth between heaven and earth. What the one lacks I supplement from the other, and in binding together, I reanimate the hesitant world, rejuvenating it in the process of change.

p. 35. Nature, in need of a master, has become my servant. If any honour remains to her, then it is due to me. What would become of the sky and the sea, the islands and the stars, and whatever lies before the eyes of men, and what would become of this silent lyre, if I did not give them voice, speech and soul! What indeed are the gods and their divine spirit unless I proclaim them!

p. 35. To be alone and without gods is death.

p. 36. O rainbow! When the spray rises in silvery clouds from the down-rushing torrent—as thou art then, such is my joy.

p. 37. I call you, slow clouds, you torrid noon-day rays, you ripe ones, from the fields, so that in you I may recognise the new day of my life. For everything has changed.

p. 41. Never had he enough words to speak of goodness, at that time, or to soothe, when he saw it, the wrath of the world. For all things are good. Then he died. Much might be said of this. And his friends saw him to the very last as he looked forth triumphantly, the most joyful of all.

p. 43. Hidden in the wood and among blossoming poppies, drowsy with sweet slumber . . .

p. 43. Abundant golden words didst thou send, happy one, with the rivers and they flow inexhaustibly into all regions.

p. 43. At the first sign he recognises perfection and, like the eagle in a thunderstorm, the bold spirit flies, prophesying, ahead of the gods who are to come.

p. 44. But we must stand under God's storm, O poets, with uncovered heads, to grasp with our own hand our Father's lightning and to proffer to the people the heavenly gift, wrapped in song.

p. 45. And the sky hangs, like an iron arch, above us, a curse paralyses the limbs of men, the gladdening gifts of Earth are like chaff, the Mother mocks us with her gifts and everything is unreal.

p. 45. Alas, our race walks in the night, it dwells as in Orcus, without divinity. Each is chained to his own concerns alone, and each hears only himself in the roaring workshop; and much do they work, the savages, with powerful arm, restlessly, but ever and ever unfruitful like the Furies remains the toil of the poor wretches.

p. 45. Hearts beat and yet speech lags behind.

p. 46. In the evening sky spring blossoms forth, numberless bloom the roses and peacefully shines the golden world; oh, thither take me, purple clouds... but as though frightened away by the foolish entreaty, the charm flies, darkness falls, and lonely under the skies, as always, I remain. Come then, gentle slumber...

p. 46. But, friend, we come too late. It is true, the gods live, but above our heads, high up, in a different world. There they are endlessly busy and seem to take little notice of our existence.

p. 46. Thus much do the gods spare us, for the weak vessel cannot always contain them. Only at times can man endure divine abundance.

p. 47. But, as I wait, I do not know what to do or say, nor do I know why there are poets in a barren age.

p. 47. But they, you say, resemble the holy priests of the wine-god who travelled from land to land in the sacred night.

p. 47. You echo him, my lyre, my song lives with him, as the spring follows the stream wherever he lists, thus I must away and follow his certain course through the mazes.

p. 48. Chose audacious ways and strove to become like the gods.

p. 49. The poetic intensity of these lines makes a verbatim prose rendering of them impossible. The following is J. B. Leishman's verse translation: Whence his speech is a shout of delight./ Not for him, as for other childern,/ To whimper in swaddling-bands;/ For as soon as the margins begin/ To creep in serpentine windings/ Towards him, and, thirstily coiling/ Around him, all heedless, would fain/ Confine him and closely preserve him/ Between their teeth, with a laugh/ He strangles them both and plunges/ On with his prey; and now, if a greater/ Does not speedily tame him,/ But lets him grow, like the lightning/ He needs must cleave the earth, and, as though bewitched,/ The woods and collapsing hills whirl fleeing behind him.

p. 49. When Father Rhine cultivates the land and nourishes children in towns which he has founded.

p. 49. All is mixed and chaotic, and primeval confusion returns.

p. 50. To make an image and to look upon the face of Christ.

p. 50. But the Father, who reigns over all, loves best the cult of the written word and the true interpretation of existing tradition. This is the rule of German song.

p. 50. But a feeling of shame prevents me from likening these worldly men to Thee.

p. 51. The poets, too, the men of the spirit, must be worldly.

p. 51. Near, and hard to grasp, is the god. Yet where there is danger, there increases salvation. Eagles dwell in the dark and the sons of the Alps cross the abysses, fearlessly, on lightly built bridges. Now, when the summits of Time are massed around us, and those we love most are near and yet wearyingly distant on furthest mountains: oh, grant us pure water, grant us wings, so that, true in spirit, we may cross over and come back.

63

p. 52. Among the Alps bright night still reigns, and clouds, creating joyful shapes, cover the yawning abyss. Hither and thither the jesting mountain air storms and tumbles; steeply down through the firs a jet of water shines and vanishes. Gradually, the chaotic mass, shuddering with joy, rushes and struggles under the rocks; youthful in body but strong, it celebrates the loving strife: fermenting and staggering within the eternal bounds, for in their midst rises the bacchantic morning. For there the year, the sacred hours, the days, grow towards infinity, in a bolder order, in a bolder array. Yet the thunder bird notes the time and high up in the air, among the mountains, he dwells and calls the day. Now, too, down below the little village awakens and, fearlessly, familiar with the sublime, looks up to the peaks, in a premonition of growth. For, like lightning, the ancient springs fall; the ground steams as they rush down. All around echo resounds and, night and day, the immense workshop is astir, proffering its gifts.

p. 53. Meanwhile the silvery heights are serenely gleaming above. And now the luminous snow is strewn with roses and higher yet, above the light, dwells the pure, blissful god, gladdened by the play of the sacred rays.

p. 54. On the hot shore the forests, drunk with thunderstorms, rustle and surge.

p. 54. And like chariots drawn by wild game, the mountains lead the way and the path hastens along.

p. 54. Now a breeze comes too and stirs the tree-tops in the grove. Look, the shadowy image of our earth, the moon, secretly comes too; the rapturous night comes, full of stars, and, it seems, little heedful of us, she shines with astounded gaze, a stranger among mankind, rising over the mountain peaks, sadly and splendidly.

p. 54. But soon, in fresh radiance, mysteriously glowing in golden vapours, with the scent of a thousand peaks, Asia, who had grown swiftly under the sun, rose before me. And, dazzled, I looked for something that I might recognise, since I was a stranger in the broad streets where the gold-crowned Pactol descends from Tmolus and where the Taurus rises and Messogis, and where the gardens, quiescent fires, are full of flowers. But high up in the light, the silvery snow blossoms, and on inaccessible walls the ancient ivy, witness of immortal life, grows, and living pillars, cedars and laurels, support the festive, the divinely built palaces.